THE AMERICAN REVOLUTION

THE HISTORY SMASHERS SERIES

The Mayflower

Women's Right to Vote

Pearl Harbor

The Titanic

The American Revolution

THE AMERICAN REVOLUTION

KATE MESSNER

ILLUSTRATED BY JUSTIN GREENWOOD

RANDOM HOUSE 🏠 NEW YORK

Text copyright © 2021 by Kate Messner
Front cover art copyright © 2021 by Dylan Meconis
Back cover art and interior illustrations copyright © 2021 by Justin Greenwood

All rights reserved. Published in the United States by Random House Children's Books, a division of Penguin Random House LLC, New York.

Random House and the colophon are registered trademarks of Penguin Random House LLC.

Visit us on the Web! rhcbooks.com

Educators and librarians, for a variety of teaching tools, visit us at RHTeachersLibrarians.com

Library of Congress Cataloging-in-Publication Data is available upon request.
ISBN 978-0-593-12046-0 (trade) | ISBN 978-0-593-12047-7 (lib. bdg.) |
ISBN 978-0-593-12048-4 (ebook)

Printed in the United States of America
10 9 8 7 6 5 4 3 2 1
First Edition

For Sarah McCarty and
her sixth-grade SMS readers

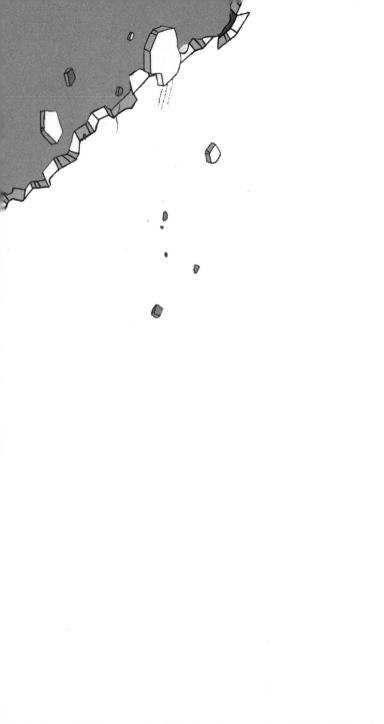

CONTENTS

You've probably heard stories about the American Revolution—how a bunch of scrappy colonists rose up to defeat the great British army and won America's independence. Maybe you've heard the tale of how Paul Revere made a midnight ride to warn all those colonial soldiers the British were coming . . . how Betsy Ross sewed the stars and stripes of the first flag for the new nation . . . how Benedict Arnold betrayed his fellow soldiers . . . or how Molly Pitcher ran out to the battlefield to take over a cannon after her husband was injured.

But really, only some of those stories are true. Some of the heroes you've read about in history books aren't so heroic when we take a closer look. Some didn't do the things they get credit for in the legends. And some weren't even real people!

Ready to smash some history? Good! Because the true narrative of the American Revolution is a lot more complicated than the myths. It's a story of flawed heroes, villains who were sometimes heroic, and unsung warriors whose names have been erased from history books. And it's the story of a nation that's still remaking itself, even today.

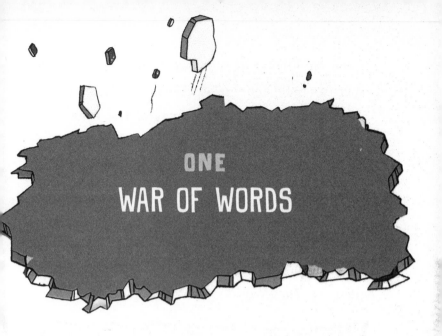

ONE
WAR OF WORDS

When Americans celebrate with cookouts and fireworks on the Fourth of July, the story of Independence Day often begins and ends with the signing of the Declaration of Independence, the document that declared the colonies would be free of British rule. But the truth is, that document wasn't

signed on July 4. And it wasn't the beginning of American independence at all—not by a long shot.

To understand the real roots of the American Revolution, you have to go way back to when the English colonies were first settled. In the 1600s, colonists arrived by the boatload. They built homes and farms on the traditional lands of Native people, or American Indians, from more than two dozen tribal nations. So the land colonists sometimes called the "New World" wasn't new at all.

The thirteen original colonies were given English names, like Virginia, New Jersey, and Maryland. But the original inhabitants of the land were Abenaki, Algonquian, Assateague, Catawba, Cherokee, Conoy, Creek, Hatteras, Haudenosaunee, Lenni-Lenape, Massachuset, Micmac, Mohegan, Nanticoke, Narragansett, Nauset, Nipmuc, Pennacook, Pequot, Powhatan, Shawnee, Susquehannock, Wampanoag, and Yamasee.

These were tribal nations whose people had lived on the continent for thousands of years. But that didn't stop the colonists from moving in and claiming the land—and everything on it—as theirs. Colonists were expected to gather up natural resources such as furs, timber, and fish, and send them back to England.

As you can imagine, Native people were upset that their traditional homelands were being invaded by Europeans who saw natural resources as something to grab and sell instead of as gifts from the Creator to share. There were conflicts, and England sent soldiers to protect the colonists from the people whose land they'd stolen.

To make matters worse, England was also fighting with France. War broke out in the colonies in 1754. It was actually a global conflict, with fighting in Europe, the Caribbean, and India, too. In America, this conflict was called the French and Indian War, since most Native tribes sided with the French.

England eventually won the war (which is why most people in the United States today speak English and not French) but ended up buried under a huge pile of debt.

It had been expensive to send all those soldiers across the ocean. England thought it was only fair that the colonists help pay for it. So the British Parliament passed a whole bunch of new laws, or acts. Some taxed the colonists, collecting money from them to help pay for all those soldiers who had defended them. Some aimed to raise money in other ways. Those laws started even before the French and Indian War.

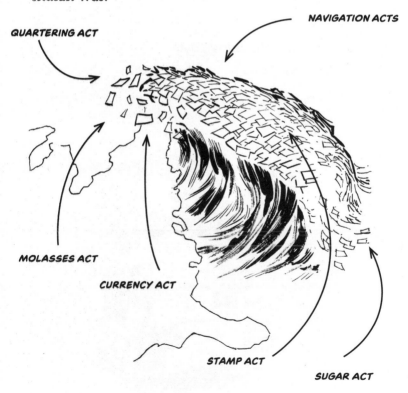

NAVIGATION ACTS

QUARTERING ACT

MOLASSES ACT

CURRENCY ACT

STAMP ACT

SUGAR ACT

The Molasses Act of 1733 had put a tax on molasses, sugar, and rum that came from non-British colonies. The colonists didn't like this, but many got around it by smuggling, or sneaking, the goods without paying the tax. England responded by setting up special offices to keep an eye out for smugglers.

The Molasses Act was one of a group of laws called the Navigation Acts, which aimed to control trade in the colonies. None of them were popular with the colonists, who preferred not to have so many rules about buying and selling goods.

After the French and Indian War, there were even more new laws. The colonists were not happy.

April 1764—The Sugar Act reduced the Molasses Act tax but ordered better enforcement. It also added taxes on certain foreign goods, such as coffee, some wines, and cloth.

September 1764—With the Currency Act, England took control of colonial money and said the colonies couldn't issue any new bills.

March 1765—The Stamp Act introduced a pile of new taxes on different kinds of paper—everything from letters and legal documents to playing cards and calendars.

March 1765—The Quartering Act required colonial governments to shelter and feed any British troops stationed in their colony. If there weren't enough barracks, soldiers could be put in stables, outbuildings, and inns.

In response to all those new laws, colonists started talking about some new ideas of their own. Representatives from nine colonies got together in New York for the Stamp Act Congress in October 1765 and passed a bunch of resolutions to protest the Stamp Act. Their rallying cry was "No taxation without representation!" Colonists argued that they couldn't be taxed by a government more than three thousand miles away—only by their own colonial governments.

Not to be outdone, England passed another new law, called the Declaratory Act, in March 1766.

Be it declared ... that the said colonies and plantations in America have been, are, and of right ought to be, subordinate unto, and dependent upon the imperial crown and parliament of Great Britain.

In other words: The colonies have to do what England says. And those resolutions the colonists passed? They don't count. Not even a little.

It wasn't long before England dropped even more taxes on the colonists, with the Townshend Revenue Act in June 1767. This was a tax on paint, oil, lead, paper, and tea, and the colonists were furious. Tensions boiled over the following summer, when British officers seized the *Liberty,* a ship owned by Boston merchant John Hancock, because they said he was smuggling wine.

Colonists were so angry that they showed up in a mob at the customs office, and the English officers there had to run for their safety. That led England to send troops to occupy Boston that fall.

The colonists fired back by setting up something called a non-importation agreement. It was a promise not to import any goods at all from Great Britain—and it meant a *lot* of lost business for England. The back-and-forth battles went on and on. Some colonists were Loyalists (also called Tories), who believed in standing up for the king of England and going along with the rules. Others were Patriots, who spoke out against the king.

So which group had the most support? For a long time, history books suggested that the colonists were pretty much equally divided in the early days of the American Revolution—one-third Patriot, one-third Loyalist, and one-third neutral.

KEEP ME OUT OF THIS.

Those estimates were based in part on a line in a letter that John Adams wrote in 1815:

I should say that full one third were averse to the revolution.

But Adams wasn't actually talking about support for the American Revolution in that letter. He was talking about American opinions on the revolution that started in France in 1789.

Today, historians believe that overall, it's more likely that Loyalists made up only about 20 percent of the population, with many more people supporting independence or trying to stay neutral.

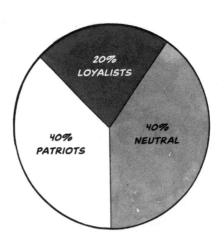

Some famous Patriots published letters in their local newspapers. This happened long before America had the First Amendment to the Constitution, which promises freedom of speech. So people used fake names to avoid being accused of treason.

JUST CALL HIM HUMPHREY PLOUGHJOGGER

More than thirty years before he'd become America's second president, John Adams was one of the most outspoken critics of the English king. In 1763, he wrote a letter to the *Boston Evening-Post* but didn't sign it with his own name. Instead, he wrote under the alias, or fake name, Humphrey

Ploughjogger. He used incorrect spellings so people might think he was an uneducated country farmer.

The grate men dos nothin but quaril with one anuther and put peces in the nues paper aginst one anuther, and sum sayes one is rite, and others sayes tuther is rite and they dont know why or wherefor.

Adams used the phony name at least three more times over the next few years. In 1783, after the Revolution was over and Britain couldn't put him on trial for treason, Adams finally admitted that he and Humphrey Ploughjogger were the same guy.

The colonists' war of words with England dragged on and on. In 1768, when the British army sent troops into Boston to protect customs officials, some residents saw that as the military occupying their town, and they didn't like it one bit. Conflicts broke out between citizens and soldiers—usually minor ones. But in March 1770, everything changed with the Boston Massacre. That's what the Patriots called the event, anyway.

ON THE NIGHT OF MARCH 5, 1770, A SCUFFLE BROKE OUT NEAR THE CUSTOMS HOUSE IN BOSTON.

WITNESSES SAY IT STARTED WITH A FEW SNOWBALLS...

...BUT IT SOON ERUPTED INTO A FULL-BLOWN RIOT. COLONISTS THREW CHUNKS OF ICE AND ROCKS AT BRITISH SOLDIERS.

AT SOME POINT, BRITISH SOLDIERS COMMANDED BY CAPTAIN THOMAS PRESTON FIRED INTO THE CROWD.

THREE COLONISTS WERE KILLED THAT NIGHT.

EIGHT WERE WOUNDED, AND TWO OF THOSE WOULD LATER DIE OF THEIR INJURIES.

THE STORY OF CRISPUS ATTUCKS

One of the men killed in the Boston Massacre was Crispus Attucks. He was multiracial, the son of a Wampanoag woman and an enslaved African man. When Attucks was about twenty-seven, he escaped from slavery and became a sailor. That was one of the few jobs a Black man could hold at the time.

According to testimony, Attucks led the group of colonists that confronted the soldiers on the night of March 5, 1770—something that would have been especially risky for a Black man who could be arrested and enslaved again. He died that night after being shot in the chest.

Samuel Adams and other Patriots made a big deal of honoring Attucks. They took his casket to Boston's city hall, where thousands of people paid their respects before his funeral.

This public display was actually more about helping the Patriots' cause than honoring a Black man who'd been killed. As someone who had escaped from slavery, Attucks would not have held a respected position in Boston society. In fact, the lawyer who defended British soldiers who were put on trial made a point to cast Attucks as the villain in the story, relying on stereotypes of Black men to make his argument. He told the jury that Attucks's "very looks was enough to terrify any person."

Later on, in the 1840s, when people in America were fighting against slavery, Attucks became a symbol of their movement. Today, multiple schools and parks are named after Attucks, honoring him as the first American to die in the Revolution.

If you look up "massacre" in the dictionary, you'll find that this word is typically used to describe the killing of a large group of defenseless people. There are more than two hundred eyewitness accounts of what happened in Boston on March 5, 1770, and many describe the colonists as the ones who started the conflict.

But that didn't stop Samuel Adams and his fellow Patriots from labeling it a massacre. They told everyone that British soldiers had fired point-blank into a crowd of innocent people. They even created art to show their side of the story.

WHAT'S WRONG WITH THIS PICTURE?

Patriot silversmith Paul Revere is usually recognized as the creator of this engraving in history books, but he actually copied it from another engraver named Henry Pelham, who created the original piece (and was seriously annoyed when Revere ended up getting all the credit).

This is still the most famous depiction of this event, but it's full of inaccuracies. How many can you spot?

The engraving shows a clear blue sky, but the riot actually happened in darkness, at about ten o'clock at night.

The art shows British soldiers lined up neatly, firing at the colonists, but witnesses say the scene was much more chaotic.

The crowd in the engraving is very well dressed, but in reality it was made up of workingmen, who probably would have looked a lot scruffier. And where are all those chunks of ice and rocks they were throwing?

It's a little hard to see, but the engraving also shows an official shooting at colonists out of the Customs House window—something that was never supported by real witnesses. Historians believe that the Patriots may have bribed, or paid off, an apprentice to say he saw that shooter so the British would look even worse.

The Pelham/Revere engraving was meant to create an emotional reaction in colonists. How could those awful British soldiers just fire into the crowd like that? People who lived in Boston were horrified—and furious.

Soon after the riot, the town of Boston published a pamphlet called *A Short Narrative of the Horrid Massacre in Boston*, which included that not-so-accurate engraving of the event.

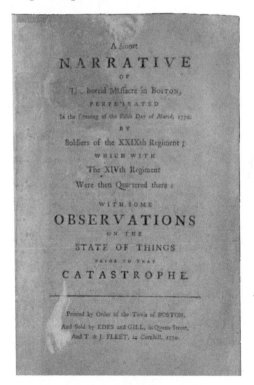

Meanwhile, British officers collected their own witness accounts and published their own description of what happened. They didn't use the word "massacre" in their pamphlet. Instead, it was called *A Fair Account of the Late Unhappy Disturbance at Boston in New England.*

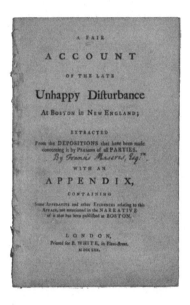

So what was it? A "horrid massacre" or an "unhappy disturbance"? The answer probably lies somewhere in between; it was really more of a skirmish—a small outbreak of fighting—than a massacre. But Samuel Adams and other Patriots did a good job getting their message out, so most people in Boston ended up calling it a massacre. Many even believed that the British had planned the whole thing ahead of time.

The British soldiers involved were put on trial for murder. Can you guess who defended them? If you guessed that it was some fancy lawyer shipped in from England, you're wrong about that. It was John Adams. Adams was a Patriot, for sure, but he also thought everybody should get a fair trial. And those British soldiers, Adams argued, had fired in self-defense.

FACTS ARE STUBBORN THINGS; AND WHATEVER MAY BE OUR WISHES, OUR INCLINATIONS, OR THE DICTATES OF OUR PASSIONS, THEY CANNOT ALTER THE STATE OF FACTS AND EVIDENCE.

In other words: I'm not on the side of the British soldiers, but that doesn't matter here. The fact is, they're not guilty.

The soldiers involved ended up being acquitted, or found not guilty, of murder, though two were convicted of the lesser charge of manslaughter. The whole mess convinced the royal governor to pull British troops out of Boston. And the acquittal made the citizens of Boston even angrier.

Maybe you're thinking this is where the Declaration of Independence comes into the story. Time to split from England, right? Time to become a new nation!

Nope. Not yet. The so-called Boston Massacre changed the way some colonists thought about their mother country, but they weren't ready to break away just yet.

TWO
TAXES, TURMOIL, AND TEA

Even after the Boston Massacre, most colonists didn't have much interest in splitting from Great Britain. They still believed they could work things out.

Stephen Hopkins, a Patriot who would eventually sign the Declaration of Independence, had expressed the views of many in 1765 when he wrote a pamphlet called *The Grievances of the American Colonies Candidly Examined.*

"Liberty is the greatest blessing that men enjoy," it starts out. Hopkins argued that colonists weren't

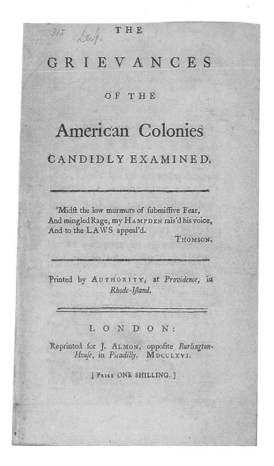

315 Dup.

THE

GRIEVANCES

OF THE

American Colonies

CANDIDLY EXAMINED,

'Midſt the low murmurs of ſubmiſſive Fear,
And mingled Rage, my HAMPDEN rais'd his voice,
And to the LAWS appeal'd.

THOMSON.

Printed by AUTHORITY, at *Providence*, in
Rhode-Iſland.

LONDON:

Reprinted for J. ALMON, oppoſite *Burlington-
Houſe*, in *Picadilly*. MDCCLXVI.

[PRICE ONE SHILLING.]

being granted their rights as British citizens, and *that* was what needed to change. Hopkins and those who agreed with him wanted Parliament to knock it off with all those taxes and get the British soldiers out of their towns. But after the Boston Massacre, things grew even more tense.

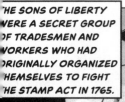

THE SONS OF LIBERTY WERE A SECRET GROUP OF TRADESMEN AND WORKERS WHO HAD ORIGINALLY ORGANIZED THEMSELVES TO FIGHT THE STAMP ACT IN 1765.

THE GROUP STARTED IN BOSTON BUT QUICKLY SPREAD THROUGH THE COLONIES.

AS TENSIONS GREW, THE SONS OF LIBERTY STEPPED UP THEIR ACTS OF PROTEST. SOMETIMES THEY WERE VIOLENT.

THEY'D BURN EFFIGIES—SIMPLE SCULPTURES THAT REPRESENTED BRITISH OFFICIALS—TO SHOW HOW MUCH THEY HATED BRITISH POLICIES. SOMETIMES THEY EVEN SET BUILDINGS ON FIRE.

BRITISH OFFICIALS KNEW ABOUT THE SONS OF LIBERTY. ONE OF THOSE OFFICIALS, LIEUTENANT WILLIAM DUDDINGSTON, HAD A REPUTATION FOR SEIZING CARGO FROM SHIPS WITHOUT ANY REAL EVIDENCE THAT LAWS HAD BEEN BROKEN.

WORD GOT OUT THAT HE WAS TARGETING THE SONS OF LIBERTY.

ON JUNE 9, 1772, DUDDINGSTON WAS PATROLLING RHODE ISLAND'S NARRAGANSETT BAY ON A BRITISH SHIP CALLED THE HMS GASPEE WHEN THE CAPTAIN OF A LOCAL BOAT LURED HIM INTO SHALLOW WATERS.

DUDDINGSTON'S SHIP RAN AGROUND.

WHEN THE SONS OF LIBERTY IN NEARBY PROVIDENCE HEARD ABOUT THAT, THEY MADE A PLAN TO TEACH DUDDINGSTON A LESSON.

THE NEXT NIGHT, DOZENS OF MEN SNUCK OUT AND SURROUNDED THE STRANDED SHIP.

THEY BOARDED THE SHIP, WOUNDED DUDDINGSTON, AND TOOK HIS CREW CAPTIVE.

DUDDINGSTON'S CREW COULD ONLY WATCH WHILE COLONISTS LOOTED AND BURNED THEIR SHIP.

It was a bold attack. The Sons of Liberty didn't wear masks or do anything else to disguise themselves. It should have been easy to find and punish them. But local court officials in Rhode Island were also pretty upset with the British. So instead of arresting the Sons of Liberty for attacking the ship, they charged Duddingston with illegally seizing goods.

When officials back in Great Britain found out about that, they were furious! They ordered that the colonists who attacked the ship be brought back to England for trial. There was just one problem: When officials arrived in Rhode Island to arrest the culprits, nobody would identify them, even though practically everyone in town knew who they were.

The Sons of Liberty were never arrested for what happened that night. But the fact that the British *tried* to arrest them and send them back to England for trial sparked outrage. Colonies created "committees of correspondence"—organizations that could share information about British actions throughout the colonies and coordinate plans to fight back. It helped the colonies communicate with one another and unite.

And then came the issue with the tea. You've probably heard stories about the Boston Tea Party—how the tax on tea made colonists so mad that they boarded ships in Boston Harbor in the middle of the night and dumped all that tea overboard. But that's not quite how it happened.

For starters, it wasn't a *new* tax on tea that upset the colonists. The Tea Act of 1773 didn't impose any new taxes at all. The Townshend Revenue Act taxes had mostly been repealed by then, but the tea tax was still in place. The 1773 law didn't add to that. It simply allowed tea sold by the East India Company to be shipped directly to the colonies and sold at a huge discount. It was designed to help the British company, which was struggling and had tons of unsold tea sitting around. The Tea Act actually made tea *less* expensive. So why were the colonists angry?

For starters, they thought England was being sneaky, offering cheap tea so they'd stop complaining about other taxes. They were also upset that this tea was being sold directly by British agents, which cut into the business of colonial merchants.

So that's what led to the Boston Tea Party, right?

Well, yes . . . but nobody called it the Boston Tea Party at the time; that phrase didn't show up until the 1820s. And tea protests weren't just a Boston thing, either. When ships full of East India Company tea arrived in New York, colonists turned them away. In Philadelphia, they threatened to tar and feather the ship's captain if he didn't take his tea and go back to England. (He heeded the warning.) In Charleston, the tea was unloaded and left to rot in the South Carolina heat.

When the ships full of tea arrived in Boston, colonists wouldn't let the sailors unload. On December 16, 1773, the Sons of Liberty led a group of men who boarded the ships and threw 342 chests of tea into the harbor. They may have heaved the smaller chests in full of tea, but historians say others were probably too heavy, so the Patriots hacked those open with hatchets and dumped them, ensuring that none of the tea would survive. It took about three hours for the group to dump about ninety thousand pounds of tea. It would have been worth more than a million dollars in today's money.

Some of the men dressed as Native people for this protest. Historians think that was partly to hide their identities—they were committing a crime, after all—and partly to send the message that they didn't consider themselves English subjects anymore. The colonists obviously didn't ask any Native people what they thought of this idea. It's hard to imagine they would have approved of men who were living on their stolen land dressing up like them to make a point about "liberty."

THOSE ROWDY BOSTONIANS

You might think uprisings like the Boston Tea Party came as a surprise—disturbing an otherwise quiet, peaceful town. But the truth is, people in Boston already had a reputation for being rowdy. There typically were riots at least once a year—most often on what was called Pope's Day, on November 5. Originally called Guy Fawkes Day, it was marked as a celebration of the defeat of a plot by some English Catholics to overthrow King James I in 1605. (One of them was named . . . you guessed it . . . Guy Fawkes.)

But little by little in Boston, this observance changed into Pope's Day, an anti-Catholic event where colonists burned effigies of the pope, the devil, and, sometimes, tax collectors, too. It was often a wild night, with fires and injuries, and there was at least one Pope's Day death. So people who went out at night to disturb the peace weren't really a novelty in Boston back then.

Guy Fawkes Day is still celebrated in England, but now it's mostly a fun night of bonfires and fireworks.

So just how big a deal was the Boston Tea Party? After it happened, colonists were divided. Some supported the Sons of Liberty, but others—including many Patriots—thought they were wrong to have destroyed all that valuable tea. Even

Benjamin Franklin, who would help lead the fight for independence, thought the East India Company should get paid for the damage.

What really pulled the colonists together wasn't the Boston Tea Party itself but the punishment England imposed a few months later, in the spring of 1774: the Coercive Acts, which the colonists called the Intolerable Acts.

Those acts closed Boston's harbor until the ruined tea was paid for and did something that angered

colonists even more: revoked the charter of Massachusetts. When the colonies were originally settled, they were granted charters from the king of England. In Massachusetts, that charter gave colonists all the rights of Englishmen. They could make their own laws and set up their own colonial governments. But when that charter was revoked, or taken away, people in Massachusetts lost rights they'd enjoyed for over a century. Suddenly, the royal governor was making all the decisions. People couldn't even hold town meetings anymore without his permission.

The new laws were meant to punish Massachusetts and to isolate the rebels there. Instead, the acts brought all thirteen colonies together. In September 1774, representatives from twelve of the colonies (all except Georgia) met in Philadelphia for the First Continental Congress and started making plans for the future. They called for new governments to be set up in Massachusetts and Virginia, where royal governors had dissolved the colonial legislatures. They also organized a boycott of British goods. People refused to buy anything made in England.

COMING TOGETHER: AMERICA'S FIRST POLITICAL CARTOON

This cartoon became a symbol of colonial unity during the American Revolution. But it had actually been published decades earlier. Benjamin Franklin first printed it in his newspaper, the *Pennsylvania Gazette*, in 1754, when he was trying to convince the colonies to come together to fight the French in the French and Indian War. In the 1770s, the cartoon was brought back, this time with the message that the colonies should unite against Great Britain. The image of a snake's body cut into different pieces suggests that none can survive on their own. It's considered to be America's first political cartoon.

Representatives of the First Continental Congress were still hoping to work things out with England, but they were also preparing for the possibility of war. Over the next year, they put out the word that colonists should get ready, too.

Volunteer units called militias formed and ran drills. George Washington, who'd commanded troops in the French and Indian War, organized men in

Virginia. In New England, "minutemen" trained to be ready at a moment's notice. The colonies sent supplies to towns near Boston, since it seemed likely the conflict might start there. By early spring in 1775, they had stockpiled enough food and gear for five thousand soldiers.

Meanwhile, across the sea, in England, British officers were having conversations of their own. They'd been considering military action against the colonies since the Boston Tea Party. Was it time to act?

One of the popular stories about the American

Revolution is about how England totally under-estimated the colonists, only to get kicked around in battle by a bunch of farmers with muskets. But that's not quite the real deal.

It's true that England didn't expect much of a war. The colonists didn't have a navy or a standing army, one made up of people whose full-time job was being a soldier. They only had militias, which were made up of volunteers. And it's true that not many of their officers were well trained. During the French and Indian War, British officers had shared some not-so-great opinions of colonial soldiers.

But British officials were concerned about how many citizen soldiers the colonies might be able to rally together. And those citizen soldiers had one big advantage: They were already in America, while the British troops would have to come on ships from more than three thousand miles away.

England had a long list of concerns about going to war. Would it be worth the money? What if France or Spain jumped in to help the colonies? What if it all blew up into a bigger war?

English officials considered all of this but decided that doing nothing would mean losing the colonies. So they made plans for war, hoping the colonists would give up after one or two big losses on the battlefield.

On April 15, 1775, British general Thomas Gage got the official order. He was told to take steps that would be:

. . . most effectual for suppressing, by a vigorous exertion of your Force, that Rebellion.

In other words: Crush that rebellion in the colonies. And get it done now.

THREE
MIDNIGHT RIDES AND THE SHOT HEARD ROUND THE WORLD

You've probably read stories about how the first battles of the American Revolution began. It's likely that Paul Revere was the hero of those tales, galloping through the countryside on a midnight ride, shouting "The British are coming!" But that beloved story has grown into a myth that needs a little smashing.

For starters, even though Paul Revere gets all the credit, he was one of many riders who sounded the warning on the night of April 18–19, 1775. British troops crossed Boston Harbor that night with two main orders.

1. *GO TO LEXINGTON AND CAPTURE REBEL LEADERS JOHN HANCOCK AND SAMUEL ADAMS.*
2. *DESTROY MILITARY SUPPLIES BEING STORED IN CONCORD.*

Dozens rode to spread the warning, but only a few—Revere, William Dawes, and Samuel Prescott—made it into history books. Most of the riders' names aren't even known.

It's unlikely that *any* of them shouted "The British are coming!" At that time, most colonists still considered themselves British citizens, too. They probably would have called the king's soldiers Redcoats or Regulars. But at least for a while, they wouldn't have been shouting anything at all. Their mission—warning Hancock and Adams—required them to reach Lexington without being caught. That meant being quiet.

It was Samuel Prescott—not Paul Revere—who managed to complete his full mission that night. He rode to Lexington, avoided capture, and went on to Concord to warn people there. Revere made it to Lexington, but British soldiers captured him later. Dawes managed to avoid getting caught, but his horse threw him off and then ran away, so Dawes ended up having to walk back to Lexington.

So why is Paul Revere the famous one? Probably because Henry Wadsworth Longfellow wrote a poem about him.

Listen, my children, and you shall hear
Of the midnight ride of Paul Revere,
On the eighteenth of April, in Seventy-Five:
Hardly a man is now alive
Who remembers that famous day and year.

Longfellow wrote this poem just before the American Civil War, thinking that a story about a good old-fashioned Patriot might lift America's spirits. That poem didn't offer a particularly accurate account of what happened back in 1775, but people liked it anyway, and Revere became known as the lone riding hero of the night. Maybe it was because his name was easiest to rhyme.

Listen up to the story of Samuel Prescott,
Who rode just like Revere but got less caught . . .

Note: Longfellow didn't write this. As far as we know, he didn't even bother trying to rhyme something with "Prescott."

Once all of the famous and not-so-famous riders had done their job, British soldiers no longer had the element of surprise on their side. Hancock and Adams fled to safety. And when the Redcoats arrived at Lexington on the morning of April 19, members of the militia were waiting for them.

The Redcoats confronted the militia. Someone fired a gun.

Who was it? Depends on who you ask. Most British accounts blamed the colonists. The colonists said it was the Redcoats, and they worked hard to get that message out in the newspapers. Massachusetts Patriots knew they'd get more support from other colonies if people believed the British soldiers had fired first. Whoever fired it, that gunshot started the American Revolution. So that shot at Lexington was the "shot heard round the world," right?

Well . . . no. That famous phrase actually comes from the poem "Concord Hymn," which was written by Ralph Waldo Emerson in the 1830s for the dedication of a monument at the North Bridge in Concord.

Here once the embattled farmers stood,
and fired the shot heard round the world.

The shots fired at Concord came after the Battle of Lexington, but Emerson didn't get asked to write a poem about that, and "shot heard round the world" sounded awfully nice. Like the famous Revere poem, this one is a little misleading when it comes to what really happened.

So Lexington was the first real battle of the Revolution, but it didn't last long. The colonists were outnumbered; there were only about eighty of them, compared to several hundred Redcoats. But they held their ground until that first shot was fired. Then chaos broke loose, and it wasn't long before the militia had to retreat. Eight militiamen were killed, and another nine or ten were injured.

WHAT'S WRONG WITH THIS PICTURE?

There were no photographers or artists at the Battle of Lexington to capture the scene for history, so all we know about it comes from the stories told by people who were there. But an artist named Amos Doolittle did paint the battle scenes a few weeks later. He went back to Lexington Green, interviewed people, and sketched out the location where the battle took place. That December, he published engravings of the battle scenes.

His engraving of the Lexington battle doesn't quite tell the real story, though. It's accurate in many ways, depicting Lexington Green with the tavern behind it as the militia retreated in chaos. But it also shows the British troops in neat lines, keeping ranks in a disciplined way. In reality, witnesses said, both groups broke ranks, and the whole scene was pretty much a hot mess. Doolittle might have taken some liberties with the trees, too. They have more leaves than usual for mid-April in chilly New England.

Only one British soldier was injured at Lexington, but it was another story when the Redcoats marched up the road to Concord. There, a hundred British soldiers faced around four hundred members of the militia. By the time the British arrived, most of the supplies they were after had already been moved. They destroyed what was left and then began to retreat, only to be chased back to Boston by a mob of militiamen who fired at them from behind every rock wall and tree stump they could find.

Casualties mounted on both sides, but the British, especially, suffered heavier losses than they'd expected.

Casualties

BRITISH	AMERICAN
73 dead	49 dead
174 wounded	39 wounded
26 missing	5 missing

Remember that idea the British had, where they hoped the colonists would call it a day after one or two losses on the battlefield? That wasn't working out so well. Lord Hugh Percy, who led the British troops back to Boston after Lexington and Concord, made that clear in the letter he wrote to London:

> *"Whoever looks upon them as an irregular mob, will find himself much mistaken."*
> —LORD HUGH PERCY, APRIL 20, 1775

In other words: These guys are better fighters than we thought.

WHO'S SINGING "YANKEE DOODLE" NOW?

STUCK A FEATHER IN HIS CAP AND

CALLED IT MACARONI . . .

As they marched to Lexington and Concord, British troops were supposedly playing "Yankee Doodle" to make fun of the colonists. No one is sure how the word "Yankee" came to describe an American, but a "doodle" was a silly person—someone from the country with no sophistication or smarts. After Lexington and Concord, though, the colonists took that song for themselves. They'd play it later on, after some of their most decisive victories of the war.

SPY ALERT!

BENJAMIN CHURCH

Both sides used spies in the Revolutionary War. The espionage started even before the first shots were fired.

Benjamin Church was a Boston surgeon and a member of the Sons of Liberty. He'd treated victims of the Boston Massacre, and on the third anniversary, he gave an emotional speech about it. He even joined a group called the Mechanics, a secret network of people who spied on the British military and Loyalists around Boston. He seemed like an amazing Patriot.

But Church had everyone fooled. He was also serving as a British spy! Historians believe it was information Church shared with the British that led to their raid on

Lexington and Concord. And then Church betrayed Paul Revere on the night of his big ride.

When Revere set off that night, his wife, Rachel, stayed in Boston. She wanted to send her husband a letter with 125 British pounds in it, in case he ended up needing money. She gave it to Church to deliver, but Church pocketed the money and handed over the letter to the British.

Later, when Rachel told Paul about that letter that never showed up, he began to suspect Church might be a spy. Patriots started keeping a closer eye on Church and eventually found a coded letter he'd delivered. After Patriot code breakers cracked it, exposing him as a spy, Church was thrown in jail. Later on, he was exiled to the West Indies, but historians believe his ship was lost at sea on the way there.

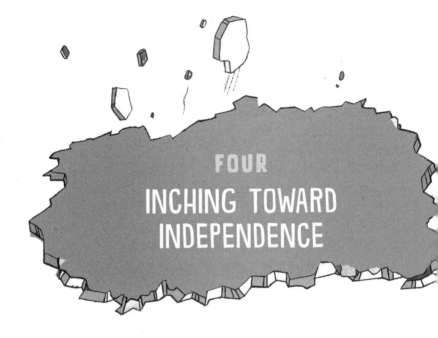

FOUR
INCHING TOWARD INDEPENDENCE

A few weeks after the battles at Lexington and Concord, there was more military action from the colonists. Two commanders—Ethan Allen and Benedict Arnold—led a raid to capture British-held Fort Ticonderoga, in New York.

Ethan Allen was in charge of a militia called the Green Mountain Boys. They once tied a Loyalist in a chair, hoisted it up a tavern signpost, and left the guy there for hours. So that tells you pretty much everything you need to know about the temperament of Allen and his group.

As for Benedict Arnold, you probably recognize that name. Wasn't he the most famous traitor in American history? He'd earn that reputation eventually. But not quite yet.

You might be wondering what Arnold was doing earlier in the siege. He was in charge, too, after all. So what did Allen's narrative have to say about how Arnold helped out? The answer is, not much. When Ethan Allen wrote the story of Fort Ticonderoga, he made himself the total star of the show and left out everybody else, including Benedict Arnold, whom he didn't like very much anyway.

However it really happened, the taking of Fort Ticonderoga was important for a couple of reasons. One was that strategic location on Lake Champlain.

Another was that Allen and Arnold managed to capture a whole bunch of cannons and other artillery along with the fort. They'd need those weapons to fight the British later on.

The next major conflict of the Revolution, the Battle of Bunker Hill, took place in June 1775. Can you guess where it happened?

If you guessed Bunker Hill, guess again. While both American and British troops had originally hoped to take Bunker Hill in Massachusetts, the fighting actually broke out at nearby Breed's Hill instead. American troops had entrenched themselves there, threatening to kick the British out of Boston. More than two thousand British soldiers rolled in and eventually fought them back. But British casualties were heavy; nearly half of their men were killed or wounded. Once again, the colonists proved they were ready to put up more of a fight than the British had hoped.

"The enemy ... advanced towards us in order to swallow us up, but they found a Choaky mouthful of us."
—LETTER FROM AMERICAN SOLDIER PETER BROWN
TO HIS MOTHER, JUNE 25, 1775

In other words: With this battle, the Redcoats bit off more than they could chew.

" I freely confess to you, when I look to the consequences in the loss of so many brave officers, I do it with horror. The success is too dearly bought."

—BRITISH GENERAL WILLIAM HOWE'S

REPORT ON THE BATTLE OF BUNKER HILL

In other words: We won, but it wasn't really worth it.

WHAT'S WRONG WITH THIS PICTURE?

John Trumbull's painting *The Death of General Warren at the Battle of Bunker's Hill* appears in many social studies books. But Trumbull gets better grades for art than for history.

It's true that Joseph Warren, a major general in the Massachusetts militia, died in the battle. But some of the people shown in this painting weren't really with him at the time. In addition, General Warren's hand is shown at his side, as if that's where he'd been shot, but somehow his uniform is still sparkling clean, white ruffled shirt and all. This helps to create the image that dying in battle is glorious and heroic.

If you look at the actual history, it's easy to

see why Trumbull chose not to show the scene more accurately. In reality, Warren died after being shot in the face with a musket, which wouldn't have made for a very nice painting.

At this point, you may be having a tough time keeping up with who was fighting and who was in charge at all these battles. Wasn't George Washington supposed to be running the show? Where was he?

Washington was actually serving in the Continental Congress as a delegate from Virginia when things were heating up around Boston. At that time, the militias all had their own leaders—often men who had some experience from the French and Indian War. But eventually the colonies realized that wasn't enough and formed the Continental Army. Washington officially took command on July 3, 1775. And the conflicts continued.

That November, Continental Army general Richard Montgomery and his troops managed to occupy Montreal, which had been held by the British. Then Montgomery and Benedict Arnold (still not a traitor) tried to take over Quebec, but their men were defeated by British forces at the end of December. Patriot forces were on the move in the South, too, attacking Loyalists in the Carolinas and Virginia.

With all these battles underway, you might be starting to wonder about the Declaration of Independence again. When would the colonists finally get around to declaring themselves a new nation?

The answer is, not yet. That was a huge step—and even after Lexington, Concord, and Bunker Hill, not all colonial leaders were ready for it.

Officially, the idea had first come up in the Second Continental Congress in May 1775, when John Rutledge from South Carolina asked about it.

DO WE AIM AT INDEPENDENCY OR DO WE ONLY ASK FOR A RESTORATION OF RIGHTS AND PUTTING OF US ON OUR OLD FOOTING?

Back then, most members decided they didn't want independence; they just wanted England to quit bossing them around. The Congress started making lists of the things America was mad about— a list of grievances—to gain support from other nations. All through 1775, they kept making requests for things to change. These were public statements, intended to reach English authorities but also meant to show the rest of the world what was happening, just in case the colonies needed help from other countries later on.

It was sort of like writing a letter to your mom and dad about why it's not fair that you have to dry the dishes every night while your little brother

watches cartoons—and then posting that letter outside for the neighbors to see, too. You don't want to leave the family. You just want them to make better rules. And you'd really like it if the neighbors were on your side.

Declaring independence wasn't an easy decision for anyone in the colonies. Even after all those battles, many still saw themselves as British citizens. Breaking away was going to be dangerous. Britain had a powerful military. And colonists had just been through the French and Indian War, so they remembered the cost of fighting.

These were all powerful arguments for trying to work things out. In fact, in January 1776, Continental Congress representative James Wilson suggested that the group make a statement saying that it did *not* want independence.

But that same month, a Patriot named Thomas Paine wrote a pamphlet called *Common Sense,* and things began to change. Paine published the pamphlet anonymously. He was afraid he'd be arrested for treason for proposing the radical idea of independence from Great Britain.

Every thing that is right or natural pleads for separation. The blood of the slain, the weeping voice of nature cries, 'TIS TIME TO PART.

People paid attention to Paine's arguments. If there had been a bestseller list back then, *Common Sense* would have been on it. Paine claimed the pamphlet sold 120,000 copies in just three months, and support for independence began to spread. Delegates to the Continental Congress went back to Philadelphia to let the others know that the idea was gaining popularity in their colonies.

Meanwhile, the battles continued, with more Patriot victories. Colonists fought off Loyalists in North Carolina and pushed back British troops in South Carolina.

And do you remember those cannons the Patriots captured when they seized Fort Ticonderoga? General Henry Knox and his men dragged them all the way to Boston. Can you imagine lugging a bunch of cannons through the snow for *three hundred miles*?

In March, George Washington's army hauled those cannons up onto a hill overlooking Boston and forced the British to evacuate the city.

And all the while, the Continental Congress was inching its way toward independence. In May 1776, the Congress passed a resolution suggesting that colonies set up their own governments to take care of their people. The introduction started like this:

Whereas his Britannic Majesty, in conjunction with the lords and commons of Great Britain, has, by a late act of Parliament, excluded the inhabitants of these United Colonies from the protection of his crown; And whereas, no answer, whatever to the humble petitions of the colonies of redress of grievances and reconciliation with Great Britain, has been or is likely to be given; but, the whole force of that kingdom, aided by foreign mercenaries, is to be exerted for the destruction of the good people of these colonies . . .

In other words: The king is doing a really rotten job taking care of the people in the colonies. He keeps ignoring our requests to fix things. And now he's fighting battles against us. So we're going to have to take care of our people on our own.

Things still didn't get any better with England, so on June 7, Richard Henry Lee of Virginia introduced new motions:

THAT THESE UNITED COLONIES ARE, AND OF RIGHT OUGHT TO BE, FREE AND INDEPENDENT STATES, THAT THEY ARE ABSOLVED FROM ALL ALLEGIANCE TO THE BRITISH CROWN, AND THAT ALL POLITICAL CONNECTION BETWEEN THEM AND THE STATE OF GREAT BRITAIN IS, AND OUGHT TO BE, TOTALLY DISSOLVED.

There was a lot of debate about this. Delegates worried that people in some colonies would never support the idea. And could the colonies possibly fight off the British army and navy? The Continental Congress was hoping for foreign aid, but what if France and Spain didn't want to help?

Those who supported Lee's motions said he was merely stating what was already true. The king of England had already made it clear that he wasn't protecting the colonists anymore. What was wrong with stating that fact?

Lee's motions weren't approved that day, but the Continental Congress appointed a committee to write up a statement—a sort of declaration—in case they decided to approve the motions later on.

So is this where we finally get to talk about the Declaration of Independence? It is! But that declaration wouldn't be written without some battles of its own.

YEARBOOK OF THE AMERICAN REVOLUTION

Here are some of the people who played a role in the early days of the American Revolution:

MOST LIKELY TO START A FIGHT

SAMUEL ADAMS was one of the earliest voices shouting about British taxes in Massachusetts. Adams helped stir up riots against the Stamp Act in Boston. He wrote dozens of newspaper letters and essays, trying to make the British look bad (and not always telling the whole truth). And while Adams didn't dump any tea into the harbor, historians are pretty sure he helped plan the Boston Tea Party.

MOST LIKELY TO FILL A WHOLE PAGE WITH HIS SIGNATURE

JOHN HANCOCK was a wealthy Boston merchant who spoke up against British taxation. Historians believe he also smuggled goods on his ships to avoid paying those taxes. Hancock served as president of the Continental Congress and was the first person to sign the Declaration of Independence, in big, bold strokes. According to legend, Hancock said he made it extra big so the "fat old king could read it without his spectacles." But there's no evidence that Hancock really said that; the quote has become famous because there's a similar line in a musical called *1776*.

MOST LIKELY TO RALLY THE TROOPS (AND BE MISQUOTED)

WILLIAM PRESCOTT commanded Patriot forces at the Battle of Bunker Hill and is often quoted as telling his men not to fire until they saw the whites of the Redcoats' eyes. But that's a legend that doesn't hold up when we check historical documents. Several soldiers who were at the Battle of Bunker Hill were quoted in an 1818 book as saying it was another officer, Israel Putnam, who actually gave that order. When Prescott wrote to John Adams two months after the battle, he didn't say anything about that specific order, but he did tell the general, "I commanded a cessation till the Enemy advanced within 30 yards, when we gave them such a hot fire that they were obliged to retire nearly 150 yards before they could Rally."

MOST LIKELY TO HOG THE LIMELIGHT

PAUL REVERE was a Boston silversmith who supported the Patriot cause and reported on the movements of British soldiers in the area. Like Samuel Adams, he helped plan the Boston Tea Party. And thanks to that poem Henry Wadsworth Longfellow wrote, Revere became the most famous of the riders who warned Lexington and Concord that Redcoats were on the way. But in many ways, the legend of Paul

Revere is bigger than the role he actually played in the Revolution.

MR. (UN)POPULARITY

JOHN ADAMS (Samuel's second cousin) was an early Patriot in Massachusetts and became a delegate for both the First and Second Continental Congresses. He was known as a great thinker but not the easiest guy to get along with. And Adams knew that—it's one of the reasons he pushed Thomas Jefferson to write the Declaration of Independence instead of writing it himself.

Adams was opposed to slavery but agreed to keep that issue out of the Declaration of Independence so the South would support it. He would go on to be the second president of the United States—the only one of the first five presidents who didn't enslave people.

MOST LIKELY TO CHANGE HIS APPEARANCE: WILL THE REAL BENJAMIN FRANKLIN PLEASE STAND UP?

BEN FRANKLIN was a Philadelphia Patriot, printer, and scientist who helped write the Declaration of Independence. He came from a poor family but liked to hang out with gentlemen, so he tried to hide his background by wearing fancy clothes and speaking in a dignified way. But once he became a big supporter of the Revolution, Franklin changed his ways and wore simpler clothes. He thought workingmen would be more likely to support the cause if they thought he was just like them.

FIVE
THE BATTLE OVER THE DECLARATION

You probably already know the name Thomas Jefferson. He was America's third president, and he usually gets all the credit for writing the Declaration of Independence. But drafting that document was a more complicated process than most history books explain.

For starters, Jefferson didn't want to write it. He wanted to go home to his plantation in Virginia, where he enslaved hundreds of people over the years, including while he was writing all those fancy words about freedom. Jefferson wanted John Adams to write the declaration. But the committee convinced

Jefferson he was a better guy for the job. He was a good writer, and people liked him more than they liked Adams, who admitted he could be pretty obnoxious sometimes. So like it or not, Jefferson was put in charge of getting a first draft together.

That's when he sat down and came up with all those brilliant ideas, right? Not quite. Jefferson actually copied a bunch of the famous document from other sources. The truth is, there wasn't just one Declaration of Independence. Colonies and towns had been adopting their own statements on independence for months. Apparently, people were tired of waiting for the Continental Congress to get around to it, so they just wrote their own.

More than ninety of these documents exist, and Jefferson borrowed language from some of them. ("Borrowed" sounds nicer than "plagiarized," right?) The Virginia Declaration of Rights, written mostly by George Mason, includes these words:

That all men are by nature equally free and independent and have certain inherent natural rights, of which, when they enter into a state of society, they cannot, by any compact, deprive or divest their posterity; namely, the enjoyment of life and liberty, with the means of acquiring and possessing property, and pursuing and obtaining happiness and safety.

Sounds a lot like this line in the Declaration of Independence, doesn't it?

We hold these truths to be self-evident, that all men are created equal, that they are endowed by their Creator with certain unalienable Rights, that among these are Life, Liberty and the pursuit of Happiness.

Jefferson used ideas from other sources, too, including the English Declaration of Rights and the writings of John Milton and John Locke, who talked about the natural rights of people.

When Jefferson finished his draft, he shared it with John Adams and Benjamin Franklin, who made suggestions for revision. Then they sent it on to the Continental Congress, where members revised a lot more. They made eighty-six changes and ended up

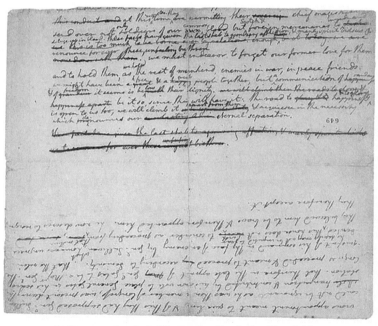

A fragment of Jefferson's first draft of the Declaration of Independence shows early revisions.

cutting about a quarter of what Jefferson had written.

Jefferson called their edits "mutilations." He'd already revised on his own and was a little prickly about the changes everybody else wanted to make.

The most controversial thing in that draft was a paragraph about slavery. It was listed as one of the complaints the colonists had about the king of England.

He has waged cruel war against human nature itself, violating its most sacred rights of life & liberty in the persons of a distant people who never offended him, captivating & carrying them into slavery in another hemisphere, or to incur miserable death in their transportation thither. this piratical warfare, the opprobrium of **infidel** *powers, is the warfare of the* CHRISTIAN *king of Great Britain. determined to keep open a market where* MEN *should be bought & sold, he has prostituted his negative for suppressing every legislative attempt to prohibit or to restrain this execrable commerce: and that this assemblage of horrors might want no fact of distinguished die, he is now exciting those very people to rise in arms among us, and to purchase*

*that liberty of which he has deprived them, &
murdering the people upon whom he also obtruded them;
thus paying off former crimes committed against the
liberties of one people, with crimes which he urges them
to commit against the **lives** of another.*

In other words: That rotten king brought people who did nothing wrong across the sea, enslaved them, and didn't care that many would die on ships on the way over. The king defends and protects the selling of human beings in the slave trade. And now, he's convinced enslaved people to rise up against us by offering them freedom if they fight for him!

That last part was a reference to a British policy that began in 1775, encouraging enslaved people to run away from Patriot enslavers to join the British.

It sure sounds like the Declaration of Independence was getting ready to do away with slavery, doesn't it?

Yeah . . . not so much. That was one of the passages that got cut from Jefferson's draft. Southern colonies like Georgia and South Carolina said there was no way they'd support a document that spoke out against slavery because they needed all that free labor for their plantations. And while some northern delegates wanted to keep that passage, others were wishy-washy about the whole thing. Northern states also benefited from the slave trade, since many ships that carried enslaved people were owned by New Englanders. In the end, the white men who made up the Continental Congress decided they wanted quick support for their declaration more than they wanted to fight for equality and freedom for everyone.

So what did Thomas Jefferson do after that passage he wrote got crossed out from the document? You might think that he'd at least have gone back to Virginia and freed the people enslaved on his own plantation. But he didn't. He kept talking about the problem of slavery and also continued to buy and sell enslaved people. Of the roughly six hundred people Jefferson enslaved in his lifetime, he ended up freeing just seven of them—two while he was alive, and five more in his will after he died.

British warships were heading for New York, ready to crush the rebellion as the Continental Congress voted to pass Richard Henry Lee's resolution for independence on July 2, 1776. Now the Continental

Army was no longer fighting for the rights of the colonists as Englishmen. They were fighting to create a new nation. Two days later, Congress approved the final text of the Declaration of Independence and sent it to the printer. That's why America celebrates Independence Day on July 4 instead of July 2, even though July 2 is when the official vote for independence took place.

JULY 4
FINAL DOCUMENT APPROVED
AND SENT TO PRINTER

July

JULY 2
INDEPENDENCE
APPROVED!

WHAT'S WRONG
WITH THIS PICTURE?

Remember that artist John Trumbull, who took some liberties with the story of the Battle of Bunker Hill? He made a painting about the Declaration of Independence, too. And once again, Trumbull wasn't too concerned with historical details.

Trumbull wasn't actually there when the Declaration of Independence was presented to the Continental Congress. When he was getting ready to make his painting years

later, he traveled around the country to talk to some of the men who were. Jefferson gave Trumbull a sketch of the room where it happened, and Trumbull used that but then added his own details. The flags and drum on the wall weren't really there, and the delegates were actually sitting in simpler chairs than those shown in the art. Trumbull fancied them up for the sake of a prettier painting.

The other problem Trumbull faced was deciding which men to include in the painting. There's no formal record of who was there when the Declaration of Independence was first presented to Congress. So what was Trumbull supposed to do about that? Should he include everybody who might have been there? Should he leave out the men who were opposed to it? Trumbull reportedly talked that question over with Jefferson and Adams and decided he'd include the men who signed the document along with those who opposed it. But then he ended up leaving out fourteen of the signers because he didn't know what they looked like.

On July 9, knowing that British warships were on the way, George Washington had the newly approved Declaration of Independence read to his army in New York City. People got so fired up that a mob tore down a statue of King George and smashed it to pieces.

Somewhere along the way, Loyalists recovered the statue's head and smuggled it back to England, but most of the monarch ended up being made into musket balls. Patriots brought the statue pieces to Connecticut, where women and children melted them down to make lead musket balls for the Continental Army. They ended up getting more than forty thousand bullets out of the statue.

ARCHAEOLOGY NOTE: MELTED MAJESTY

The Museum of the American Revolution shares a quote from an American who commented on the melting down of the king's statue, saying that the king's troops would have "melted Majesty fired at them." And modern science was able to prove that guy was right! Archaeologists who tested musket balls found at the site of the Battle of Monmouth, in New Jersey, discovered that the combination of lead and tin in those musket balls was an exact match with the composition of the remaining pieces of that King George statue.

As word spread about the Declaration of Independence, ideas about freedom caught fire with more and more people. But not always in the way the document's authors had intended. Five years after the Declaration of Independence was signed, an enslaved Massachusetts woman known as Mumbet filed a lawsuit to fight for her freedom.

Some stories say she was inspired by the words of the Declaration of Independence, or by the Massachusetts Constitution, which also says that all men are born equal, with rights that can't be taken away. Mumbet won her freedom and took a new name for herself, Elizabeth Freeman. Her case and others like it led the Massachusetts Supreme Court to outlaw slavery in the state in 1783.

SPY ALERT!
HERCULES MULLIGAN

Just days before the Declaration of Independence was approved, a Patriot spy learned of a British plan to kill George Washington. That spy was Hercules Mulligan, an Irish tailor who worked in New York City, making fancy clothes for people from both sides of the conflict.

Mulligan made it a habit to be super-friendly when Loyalists showed up. He'd give them drinks (sometimes a *lot* of drinks!) to get them talking. And in June 1776, New York's Loyalist mayor spilled a big secret. He told Mulligan the British were planning to pay American troops to betray General Washington. They'd talked about kidnapping him and supposedly had a backup plan, to poison one of his favorite meals—ham, lettuce, and buttered peas.

It was set to happen in just a few days, so as soon as the mayor left, Mulligan headed for Washington's headquarters to share what he'd heard. On the way, he met Alexander Hamilton, who carried the news to Washington.

The Patriots discovered which of Washington's guards were involved in the plot, hanged one of them, and threw the others in prison. After that, Mulligan became a regular spy for the Continental Army and ended up foiling another plot to kill the general, in 1781.

SIX

THE SPIRIT OF '76

You might think that the Declaration of Independence inspired colonists from all walks of life to enlist in the Continental Army. And it did . . . for a while, anyway. But it wasn't long before reality set in. Military service was hard and dangerous. And as time passed, fewer men enlisted on their own, so the Continental Army had to start offering incentives, such as clothing, blankets, and extra cash. There were deals for shorter enlistments than the usual year of service and, eventually, promises of land for those who enlisted for three years. But there was still a question of just *who* was allowed to serve their country.

Many African American soldiers were part of colonial militias. They'd served in the French and Indian War and fought heroically at Lexington, Concord, and the Battle of Bunker Hill. But when George Washington took command of the Continental Army, he brought some racist ideas along from his Virginia plantation. Soon after taking command, Washington decided that no more Black soldiers would be allowed to enlist, but those already serving would be allowed to stay. Then, in November 1775, the Continental Congress declared that all Black people were ineligible to serve.

FIGHTING FOR FREEDOM

The truth is, Black Americans were fighting for freedom long before the American Revolution began. They organized their own revolts throughout the colonies.

In September 1739, enslaved people in South Carolina marched with banners calling for liberty. The protesters killed the owners of a local gun shop, gathered up weapons, and killed more than twenty other white people, in what's come to be called the Stono Rebellion. When the governor ordered that the rebellion be crushed, half of the protesters were killed, and the others arrested.

That wasn't the only story of revolt. Enslaved people rose up in Manhattan in 1712. Another group plotted to seize the Maryland city of Annapolis in 1740. And there were numerous uprisings in the West Indies. Stories of these rebellions fed colonists' fears about enslaved people and probably contributed to the ban on Black soldiers serving in the army, even though troops were desperately needed.

The same month the Congress banned African American men from serving in the Continental Army, England did just the opposite. The Earl of Dunmore, who was also the royal governor of Virginia, issued a proclamation urging enslaved men to run away from Patriot masters and join the British army. Hundreds of those men became part of the Royal Ethiopian Regiment. Dunmore gave them uniforms embroidered with the words "Liberty to Slaves" and promised they'd be freed after the British won the war.

That was a huge problem for Washington, who was already having a tough time holding on to soldiers. In a letter to Richard Henry Lee, he said Dunmore had to be crushed, or else . . .

... he will become ... the most formidable Enemy America has—his strength will Increase as a Snow ball by Rolling; and faster, if some expedient cannot be hit upon to convince the Slaves and Servants of the Impotency of His designs.

In other words: We're in big trouble if we can't convince enslaved people to stop signing up to help this guy!

It probably won't surprise you to know that Washington's rule against African Americans serving in battle didn't last long. Military leaders decided having soldiers was more important than hanging on to racist ideas about who should be a soldier. At the end of 1775, Washington did a total turnaround and ordered that Black men could, in fact, be recruited for the Continental Army. Those new soldiers would play a crucial role in the next battles of the Revolution.

Remember those British ships that were heading for New York City as the Declaration of Independence was being written? They arrived in August 1776 and seized Brooklyn. Washington's army was trapped and would have been wiped out if it weren't for some of those Black soldiers, who were part of a unit called the Marblehead Mariners.

ON AUGUST 28, WASHINGTON'S TROOPS HAD BATTLED ALL DAY. WHEN DARKNESS FELL ON THAT STORMY NIGHT, THEY WERE SOAKING WET AND TRAPPED.

BUT WASHINGTON HAD A SECRET ESCAPE PLAN. HE'D ORDERED HIS MEN TO SEIZE ALL THE SMALL FLAT-BOTTOMED BOATS IN THE AREA.

THE WIND THAT NIGHT KEPT BIG BRITISH SHIPS FROM MOV INTO THE EAST RIVER. SMALLER BOATS COULD STILL OPERATE. BUT WOULD IT BE POSSIBLE TO MOVE AN ENTIR ARMY TO SAFETY BEFORE THE BRITISH DISCOVERED THEN

"To move so large a body of troops, with all their necessary appendages, across a river full a mile wide, with a rapid current, in face of a victorious, well-disciplined army, nearly three times as numerous . . . , and a fleet capable of stopping the navigation, so that not one boat could have passed over, seemed to present most formidable obstacles."
—FROM THE MEMOIR OF COLONEL BENJAMIN TALLMADGE

THE PLAN WAS TOP SECRET. THE SOLDIERS WEREN'T EVEN TOLD WHAT WAS HAPPENING UNTIL IT WAS TIME FOR THEM TO GET IN THE BOATS.

THE MARBLEHEAD MARINERS, LED BY JOHN GLOVER, WERE PUT IN CHARGE OF THE MISSION. THEY WERE NEW ENGLAND SAILORS AND INCLUDED A NUMBER OF AFRICAN AMERICAN AND NATIVE MEN. ANOTHER UNIT FROM MASSACHUSETTS HELPED OUT, TOO.

NO LIGHTS. NO SOUND. THAT WAS THE ORDER.

BACK AND FORTH, THE MARINERS ROWED IN THE DARKNESS.

THE MISSION HAD TO BE COMPLETED BEFORE DAWN. IF THE BRITISH FOUND OUT, THEY'D ATTACK AND TAKE PRISONER ANYONE WHO HADN'T MADE IT ACROSS.

JUST BEFORE MIDNIGHT, THE WINDS TURNED AND MADE IT EVEN HARDER TO NAVIGATE.

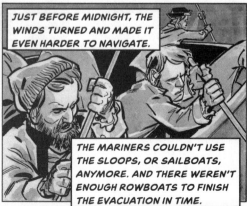

THE MARINERS COULDN'T USE THE SLOOPS, OR SAILBOATS, ANYMORE. AND THERE WEREN'T ENOUGH ROWBOATS TO FINISH THE EVACUATION IN TIME.

EVENTUALLY THE WIND SHIFTED AGAIN, SO THE SLOOPS COULD BE USED ONCE MORE.

BUT OFFICERS FEARED THEY'D ALREADY LOST TOO MUCH TIME.

WHEN DAWN BROKE, PART OF THE ARMY'S REAR GUARD WAS STILL STRANDED ON LONG ISLAND.

LUCKILY, A THICK MORNING FOG HID THEM UNTIL THEY COULD BE EVACUATED, TOO.

THE MISSION WAS A SUCCESS. IN LESS THAN NINE HOURS, THE MARINERS FERRIED NINE THOUSAND MEN TO SAFETY!

EVERY SOLDIER MADE IT TO THE OTHER SIDE, ALONG WITH THEIR HORSES, GUNS, AND SUPPLIES. ONLY A FEW CANNONS HAD TO BE LEFT BEHIND.

The Continental Army had escaped to fight another day! But the next battles didn't go so well. Between August and November 1776, the British took western Long Island, Manhattan, Staten Island, and more of the Hudson Valley.

SPY ALERT!
NATHAN HALE

You've probably heard the name Nathan Hale. He's the most famous spy of the American Revolution—and probably the most famous in American history. So he must have been really great at his job, right?

Actually, not so much. This is one of those myths that needs a bit of smashing.

The truth is, Hale was kind of a terrible spy. That wasn't entirely his fault, since he didn't get much training. People who knew Hale said he was a crummy liar and trusted people way too much. He also broke a ton of spy rules, talking to people about his plans and even traveling with identification that included his real name.

So it's not surprising that Hale got caught not long after he volunteered for his first real spy mission. In September 1776, Hale was sent to Long Island, where he pretended to be a Loyalist teacher fleeing from Patriots. He told people he needed a job in a place where there were more Loyalists like him. He was supposed to use that time to learn about British general William Howe's plans to take New York.

Hale did manage to slip behind British lines and collect information, but New York fell before he had a chance to deliver it. Then Hale got caught while he was trying to get back to American-controlled territory. The British searched him, found his notes and drawings, and delivered him to General Howe, who ordered him to be hanged the next day.

Even though Hale wasn't a very successful spy, he's still remembered as a hero, probably because he was the first American to be executed for serving his country in that way. His real contribution to history might be that George Washington learned from all the mistakes of the Nathan Hale mess and got better at running spy rings later on in the war.

In October 1776, Benedict Arnold (still not a traitor!) was commanding a small American fleet on
Lake Champlain, which the British were hoping to
seize. Arnold knew his quickly assembled gunboats
probably couldn't hold off the British navy on the
wide part of the lake, but he thought he might have a
chance if he could engage those big ships in a narrow
channel instead. So Arnold tucked his ships behind
Valcour Island and waited there for the British, who
were expected to sail down from Canada.

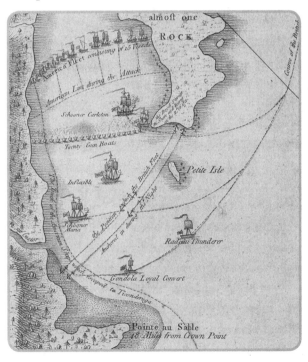

When the British ships finally showed up, Arnold sent a couple of his boats out to lure them into the channel, and the Battle of Valcour Island began. Arnold's men held their own for a while, but by the time the sun went down, it was clear the British would be able to finish them off in the morning.

But Arnold had one more trick up his sleeve. He'd had his men take soundings, measuring the depth of the water all along the New York shore. So even though the British ships had lined up to block his escape route to the south, he figured out that there was still room to sneak away.

Arnold ordered his sailors to line the gunboats up single file. He told them to wrap their oars with cloth so they wouldn't make any noise. And he had them set up a lantern in the back of each boat, shrouded on three sides so it could be seen only by the vessel behind it. That night, while the British celebrated their upcoming victory, Arnold's boats slipped away into the darkness. The British chased them down the next day and ultimately won the battle. But some historians believe Arnold's fleet delayed the British enough that they decided to hole up at Crown Point for the winter instead of continuing south, down the lake.

Meanwhile, after being battered by the British in New York, George Washington had retreated with his troops into Pennsylvania. By December, things were not looking good at all. Washington's army was falling apart. They'd suffered heavy losses, and most of the soldiers' enlistments were about to run out. Washington feared that what was left of his army would simply call it a day and walk home at the end of the month.

Thomas Paine, the guy who wrote *Common Sense*,

had joined the Continental Army, and that month, he published another pamphlet, called *The American Crisis*. It urged colonists to join the fight instead of giving up.

> "These are the times that try men's souls: The summer soldier and the sunshine patriot will, in this crisis, shrink from the service of their country; but he that stands by it *NOW*, deserves the love and thanks of man and woman."

That helped a little, at least. Nobody wanted to be a wimpy "summer soldier." But Washington still faced the threat of British troops. He'd ordered his men to seize every boat they could find so the British couldn't follow them across the Delaware River and attack. But winter was setting in. Soon the river would freeze, and then the Redcoats would be able to walk across and wipe out what was left of Washington's troops.

Washington was running out of time. On December 18, he wrote a letter to his brother, explaining that things had taken "an adverse turn."

You can form no Idea of the perplexity of my Situation. No Man, I believe, ever had a greater choice of difficulties and less means to extricate himself from them.

In other words: There's pretty much no way out of this mess.

Washington needed a miracle.

SEVEN

SNOWSTORMS, SPIES, AND THE ELEMENT OF SURPRISE

The day after George Washington wrote that boy-are-we-in-big-trouble letter to his brother, there was a snowstorm. Temperatures dropped. Washington knew it was just a matter of time before the Delaware River would freeze. And British general William Howe's plans were clear. The Patriots had intercepted a letter Howe wrote to a friend on December 21, saying the British planned to attack as soon as the ice was solid enough to cross.

Washington didn't have much time. But he had an idea. On the night of December 22, he gathered some of his officers and told them the plan. They'd march with more than two thousand soldiers on Christmas night, cross the river, and attack the town of Trenton, New Jersey, before dawn.

THE HESSIANS AT TRENTON

Trenton was occupied by Hessians, hired German soldiers who fought for the king of England. They had a reputation as fierce fighters and were feared by soldiers in the Continental Army. Hessian soldiers even earned a line in the Declaration of Independence, on that list of grievances against the king.

He is at this time transporting large Armies of foreign Mercenaries to compleat the works of death, desolation and tyranny.

About fourteen hundred Hessians were occupying Trenton that December. In reality, they weren't all that different from any other soldiers. Many had been lured to America with promises of wealth. They even sang a song about that in the taverns sometimes.

Go with us to America.
There will be enough for all.
There will be silver, gold, and money.
Everything that man seeks in the world
All that a man seeks there
Is in America.

It's mostly a myth that Hessian soldiers were bigger and scarier than other troops. Probably their tall, pointy hats helped with that reputation. But most of the twenty thousand Hessians who fought with the British were poor farmers with families. And some were just boys. Private Johannes Reuber, who was seventeen years old, was part of the regiment stationed at Trenton with Colonel Johann Rall and was taken as a prisoner of war after Washington's attack.

On Christmas morning, Washington's army went about its business as if nothing were planned. The chaplains led religious services, and the usual drills took place.

But behind the scenes, soldiers were issued blankets and ammunition. The women who worked the mess tents prepared three days' worth of food for the upcoming march to Trenton. Early that afternoon, the troops assembled and started marching toward McConkey's Ferry, where they would cross the Delaware River.

Remember all those boats Washington had ordered his men to seize? It was time to put them into action. And once again, Black sailors came to the rescue of the general who had decided a year earlier that they were unfit to serve in his army. The Marblehead Mariners were put in charge of ferrying all those soldiers—twenty-four hundred men—and their supplies across the river in the dead of night.

THE PLAN HAD BEEN TO START AT DUSK, BUT ICE FLOES IN THE RIVER CAUSED A DELAY.

FINALLY, THE MISSION BEGAN! A FULL MOON MADE IT EASIER FOR THE MEN TO SEE AS THEY LOADED THE BOATS.

EACH BOAT COULD CARRY ABOUT FORTY SOLDIERS PACKED TIGHTLY TOGETHER. THEY'D BEEN BUILT TO CARRY IRON AND GRAIN—NOT MEN.

THE MARBLEHEAD MARINERS USED POLES TO PUSH THROUGH THE SHALLOW WATERS NEAR SHORE, THE SWITCHED TO OARS AS THE RIVER GREW DEEPER.

THE SAILORS FERRIED BOATLOAD AFTER BOATLOAD OF SOLDIERS ACROSS TO NE JERSEY. THEY'D PLANNED TO BE MARCHING BY MIDNIGHT.

THE HULLS OF THE BOATS WERE PAINTED BLACK TO MAKE THEM HARD TO SEE IN THE DARK.

BUT WHAT IF HESSIAN GUARDS WERE WAITING ON THE OTHER SIDE OF THE RIVER?

BUT THE CROSSING WAS TREACHEROUS HUGE CHUNKS OF ICE BARRELED DOWN TH RIVER AND SLAMME INTO THE BOATS.

IT WAS TAKIN TOO LONG.

BY THEN, SOME MEN REALIZED THEIR MUSKETS WERE TOO WET TO FIRE. THEY SENT WORD UP TO THE FRONT. AND THE REPLY CAME BACK.

THEY FIXED THEIR BAYONETS, TH[E] SHARP BLADES THAT WENT ON MUSKETS FOR FIGHTING IN CLOS[E] QUARTERS, AND CONTINUED ON.

ADVANCE AND CHARGE!

WHEN THE TROOPS FINALLY REACHED TRENTON, IT WAS IN DAYLIGHT, BUT SOMEHOW THEIR ATTACK HAD STAYED A SURPRISE.

DER FEIND! HERAUS!

THE FIGHTING LASTED ONLY ABOUT AN HOUR.

BY THE TIME IT WAS OVER, WASHINGTON'S TROOPS HAD KILLED SOME TWENTY HESSIAN SOLDIERS, WOUNDED ABOUT A HUNDRED MORE, AND TAKEN ABOUT A THOUSAND AS PRISONERS.

A FEW OF WASHINGTON'S SOLDIERS DIED OF EXPOSURE BECAUSE OF THE AWFUL WEATHER, BUT HE DIDN'T LOSE A SINGLE MAN IN THE BATTLE.

WHAT'S WRONG WITH THIS PICTURE?

This famous painting takes up an entire wall in New York City's Metropolitan Museum of Art. But German artist Emanuel Leutze, who painted the scene seventy-five years after it happened, didn't get all the details right.

For starters, Leutze painted the wrong kind of boat. Durham boats, used to ferry most of Washington's men across the Delaware, were bigger than this and could carry more men. The oars and poles the Marble-head Mariners used to maneuver those boats were eighteen feet long, a lot longer than the ones depicted in the painting. And that nice American flag shown on the boat? It actually wasn't in use yet.

Finally, see the way George Washington is posing in the front of the boat, as if he's just waiting for some famous artist to paint him? Given the wind and the storm that night, and the way chunks of ice were slamming into the boats, there's no way Washington would have crossed like that. If he'd tried, he probably would have ended up toppling into the river.

SPY ALERT!

JOHN HONEYMAN?

There were spies running rampant on both sides in the days leading up to the Battle of Trenton. So Washington wrote to his officers, asking them to find somebody to gather intel on the Hessians. He requested:

> . . . some person who can be engaged to cross the River as a spy, that we may, if possible, obtain some knowledge of the Enemy's situation, movements, and Intention. Particular enquiry should be made by the person sent, if any preparations are making to cross the river; whether any Boats are building and where, whether any are coming across Land from Brunswick, whether any great collection of Horses are made, and for what purpose. Expence must not be spared in procuring such Intelligence, and will readily be paid by me.

In other words: Find somebody to go spy on the Hessians. Find out if they're making plans, building boats, or rounding up horses. Doesn't matter how much it costs. I'm paying.

According to local stories, Washington *may* have ended up getting help from a New Jersey butcher named John Honeyman. After the war, Honeyman's family told stories about how he'd visited taverns, talked with people around town, and reported back to Washington about the number of troops and defenses. There are no documents to support the family's stories, though. Might that be because Washington was getting smarter by then and leaving less of a paper trail about the men he enlisted as spies? Maybe. But it's also possible that the Honeyman spy story is another myth.

Washington most certainly had people feeding him information, though, and so did the Hessians. In fact, Colonel Rall might have had a better warning about the attack on Trenton if he'd been paying more attention to his spies. Two Loyalist brothers supposedly saw Washington's troops getting ready to cross the river and went to warn Rall. But the Hessian commander was at a party and refused to talk to them, so they wrote him a note instead. Rall was reportedly busy playing cards, so he shoved it into his pocket, unread.

EIGHT
SMALLPOX AND SARATOGA

After the surprise victory over the Hessians at Trenton, Washington's troops went on to beat the British at the Battle of Princeton on January 3, 1777. Then his troops set up camp for the winter in Morristown, New Jersey.

It was a rough few months. There wasn't enough food or clothing. Soldiers had only promised to serve for a certain amount of time, and many were leaving as soon as that time was up. Others simply deserted and walked away. Within weeks, Washington had lost at least a third of the men who'd promised to stay through the winter. On top of all that, disease was spreading through the community and the army.

AN INVISIBLE ENEMY

In the early days of the American Revolution, more Continental soldiers died from disease than from enemy bullets, and smallpox was the deadliest. The virus swept through the troops, with outbreaks in both Boston and Philadelphia in 1776. Smallpox devastated Continental troops in Quebec and was one of the reasons they had to retreat.

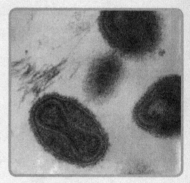

Smallpox virus, seen under a transmission electron microscope

George Washington, who'd had smallpox when he was a teenager, understood the threat it posed to his army. So that winter in

Morristown, he wrote a letter to army doctor William Shippen and made arrangements for the troops to be inoculated. (Inoculation was an early form of vaccination.)

Finding the Small pox to be spreading much and fearing that no precaution can prevent it from running through the whole of our Army, I have determined that the troops shall be inoculated. This Expedient may be attended with some inconveniences and some disadvantages, but yet I trust in its consequences will have the most happy effects. Necessity not only authorizes but seems to require the measure, for should the disorder infect the Army in the natural way and rage with its usual virulence we should have more to dread from it than from the Sword of the Enemy.

Not everyone agreed with Washington's inoculation plan, because the idea was still new. It involved infecting people with a live form of the virus so they'd get a milder form of the disease and then be immune to it. Today's vaccinations are much safer and more comfortable (most no longer use live viruses or make people feel sick at all), and they're even more effective in fighting disease. But Washington's plan worked. After that winter, the Continental Army stopped losing so many soldiers to smallpox.

When the snow finally melted, the battles heated up again. Some went the Patriots' way, and some didn't. Benedict Arnold (nope—still not a traitor!) led his men to push back British troops in Ridgefield, Connecticut, in April 1777. And that August, when British troops at Fort Stanwix, New York, found out Arnold was on his way, they retreated, too. (Not bad work for a guy who's getting ready to betray his new country, right?)

American forces also won the Battle of Bennington, Vermont, in August.

Can you guess which state that battle was fought in? If you figured this was a trick question and it wasn't Vermont, congratulations! The Battle of Bennington was actually fought in Walloomsac, New York, a few miles over the state line.

In other battles that summer, the British were victorious. In July, they took back Fort Ticonderoga.

In August, they defeated the Patriots at the Battle of Oriskany, also in New York, and in September, they won the Battle of Brandywine, in Pennsylvania, one of the bloodiest conflicts of the whole war.

And there was no rest for the weary. Just days later, the troops were ready to clash again nearby, at what's come to be known as the Battle of the Clouds. And for good reason . . .

As the battle was starting, the skies opened up and rain came down in buckets. Washington was outnumbered and knew his men's muskets wouldn't fire in all that rain, so he retreated.

A NEW FLAG FOR A NEW NATION

Amid all the battles of 1777, the Continental Congress approved a resolution to adopt a new flag for the United States of America:

> *Resolved, that the Flag of the thirteen United States shall be thirteen stripes, alternate red and white; that the Union be thirteen stars, white on a blue field, representing a new constellation.*

The Birth of Old Glory, painted by Percy Moran, 1917

This painting is meant to show the historic moment when Betsy Ross, who is known for sewing America's first flag, got to show her handiwork to General George Washington himself. There's just one problem. None of that really happened.

Congress did approve a new flag in June 1777, but there are no primary sources to suggest that the Philadelphia seamstress named Betsy Ross had anything to do with it. There are no documents or notes from Washington's journals. No receipts or anything else.

Pretty much nobody had heard of Betsy Ross back then. But almost a hundred years later, her grandson wrote a paper for the Historical Society of Pennsylvania, claiming that his grandmother made the first flag. When that story was published, Americans loved it! They loved it so much that nobody bothered to ask for proof that it was true. The legend of Betsy Ross spread, and the story now appears in a lot of history books.

Is it possible that Betsy Ross sewed that first flag? Sure. She is known to have sewn flags for the Pennsylvania navy. Historical records support that. But there's nothing but family lore to suggest the story of Ross sewing America's first flag is anything but a well-loved legend.

By the end of September 1777, British troops were occupying Philadelphia. They'd been aiming to seize the headquarters of the Continental Congress, but Patriot leaders had been smart enough to leave town the week before, moving their operations to Lancaster and then York, Pennsylvania.

SPY ALERT!

LYDIA BARRINGTON DARRAGH

When British troops occupied Philadelphia in 1777, they took over a bunch of homes, including the one where Lydia Barrington Darragh lived with her family. British officers used the Darraghs' parlor for strategy meetings.

At first, the British told Lydia Darragh she needed to leave when they wanted to use her house. She said no way, because she was busy and had kids to take care of. Darragh complained to her cousin, who was a British officer, and he took her to see General Howe. Howe assumed Darragh was a Loyalist and said fine, she could stay in her house. But his men were going to meet in her parlor anyway.

So that's what happened. And when British officers met to talk strategy, Lydia Darragh listened in on their conversations. At first, she tried to be sneaky about it, but it turned out that the officers didn't really care if she was around. After a while, they even invited her in to serve refreshments during their secret meetings.

Early that December, the British officers told Darragh they had an especially important meeting and there could be no interruptions. They told her to stay in her bedroom. But instead, she snuck into a storage closet near the parlor to eavesdrop. There, she learned that British forces were planning to attack Continental troops camped northwest of Philadelphia.

Darragh knew she had to tell someone, so she asked for a pass to leave the city to buy flour. She went alone and didn't even tell her husband where she was going. After she dropped off her flour sack to be filled, she went out to find an American patrol and pass along her news, which made it to General Washington. When the British attacked, they found Washington's troops dug in and ready to fight. After some skirmishes, the British decided to call it a day and went back to Philadelphia.

The Continental Army was in a tough spot. The Americans were suffering too many losses, and they needed help. They were counting on the French to join their fight. They hoped Benjamin Franklin might be able to convince them.

Franklin had been sent to Europe in 1776 to try to gain French support for the Revolution. So far, though, France was reluctant to get too involved. The Americans needed a real win—a more decisive victory to show France that they were up for the fight. That came at the Battles of Saratoga, in New York, in the fall of 1777.

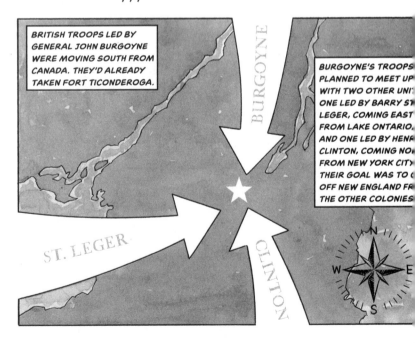

BRITISH TROOPS LED BY GENERAL JOHN BURGOYNE WERE MOVING SOUTH FROM CANADA. THEY'D ALREADY TAKEN FORT TICONDEROGA.

BURGOYNE

BURGOYNE'S TROOPS PLANNED TO MEET UP WITH TWO OTHER UNIT ONE LED BY BARRY ST LEGER, COMING EAST FROM LAKE ONTARIO, AND ONE LED BY HENR CLINTON, COMING NOI FROM NEW YORK CITY THEIR GOAL WAS TO OFF NEW ENGLAND FR THE OTHER COLONIES

ST. LEGER

CLINTON

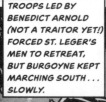

TROOPS LED BY BENEDICT ARNOLD (NOT A TRAITOR YET!) FORCED ST. LEGER'S MEN TO RETREAT, BUT BURGOYNE KEPT MARCHING SOUTH . . . SLOWLY.

BURGOYNE'S TROOPS WOULD HAVE BEEN QUICKER IF THEY HADN'T BEEN HAULING SO MANY SUPPLIES. BURGOYNE'S WAGON TRAIN STRETCHED ON FOR A MILE. HE WASN'T KNOWN FOR TRAVELING LIGHT.

BURGOYNE WAS KNOWN BY THE NICKNAME GENTLEMAN JOHNNY BECAUSE HE LOVED FANCY THINGS. HE WASN'T BIG ON ROUGHING IT IN THE AMERICAN WILDERNESS AND INSISTED ON BRINGING EVERYTHING HE THOUGHT HE NEEDED TO BE COMFORTABLE, INCLUDING CASES OF CHAMPAGNE.

AMERICAN GENERAL HORATIO GATES KNEW THAT BURGOYNE WAS COMING AND USED ALL THAT TIME TO BUILD DEFENSES AT A PLACE CALLED BEMIS HEIGHTS.

FROM THERE, A CANNON COULD REACH BRITISH SHIPS ON THE HUDSON RIVER OR TROOPS MARCHING ON THE ROAD NEARBY.

ON SEPTEMBER 19, BURGOYNE SPLIT HIS ARMY INTO THREE COLUMNS AND MARCHED TOWARD THE AMERICAN TROOPS. FIGHTING BROKE OUT AROUND NOON AT A PLACE CALLED FREEMAN'S FARM.

THE BATTLE WAS FIERCE. AMERICAN FORCES WOULD TAKE THE FIELD ONLY TO LOSE IT AGAIN. THE ADVANTAGE SWUNG BACK AND FORTH FOR HOURS.

BY THE END OF THE DAY, AMERICAN FORCES HAD TO RETREAT. BRITISH TROOPS HELD THE FIELD BUT COULDN'T ADVANCE ANYMORE.

AMERICAN TROOPS HAD LOST THE FIELD, BUT THE BRITISH SUFFERED TWICE AS MANY CASUALTIES.

BURGOYNE WAS STILL WAITING FOR TROOPS TO ARRIVE FROM NEW YORK TO BACK HIM UP. THEN HE'D BE ABLE TO CRUSH THE CONTINENTAL ARMY! HE WAITED . . . AND WAITED. . . .

BUT THOSE TROOPS NEVER SHOWED UP. GENERAL HOWE HAD ORDERED THEM TO TURN AROUND TO HELP DEFEND PHILADELPHIA INSTEAD.

ON OCTOBER 7, BURGOYNE COULDN'T WAIT ANY LONGER. WINTER WAS COMING, AND SUPPLIES WERE LOW. HE SENT 1,500 MEN OUT TO GATHER INFORMATION ON THE AMERICAN TROOPS.

BUT AMERICAN TROOPS WERE ON THE MOVE, TOO. A UNIT OF 13,000 MEN ATTACKED BURGOYNE'S TROOPS, KILLED ONE OF THEIR FAVORITE GENERALS, AND PUSHED THE BRITISH BACK.

THE BRITISH RETREATED BEHIND TWO REDOUBTS, OR BARRIERS.

AMERICAN FORCES PUSHED ON AND SEIZED ONE OF THE REDOUBTS, FORCING THE BRITISH TO RETREAT.

BURGOYNE'S MEN RETREATED TO THE TOWN OF SARATOGA, WHERE THEY SET UP CAMP, HOPING TO STAGE ANOTHER ATTACK. BUT IN TWO DAYS, THEY WERE SURROUNDED.

BURGOYNE SURRENDERED ON OCTOBER 17.

BENEDICT ARNOLD (STILL NOT A TRAITOR!) AT SARATOGA

There's a great story about Benedict Arnold at the Battles of Saratoga. He was still fighting on the side of the Patriots then but was starting to feel a little salty about being passed over for promotions. He also couldn't stand his commanding officer, General Horatio Gates, and argued with him a lot. That's well documented.

What's not so well documented is just what role Arnold played in the Battles of Saratoga. Many books describe how even though Gates had removed Arnold from his command, Arnold busted out of his tent to lead his men into battle at Bemis Heights.

With that dramatic quote, the story goes, Arnold jumped on his horse and stormed into the middle of the fighting, shouting and cursing and rallying the troops. But the books that have Arnold uttering those heroic words cite just one source—a biography about Benedict Arnold that was written by one of his relatives more than a hundred years after the battle.

However it happened, Arnold did end up in the middle of the fighting that day and was wounded. First, he was shot in the leg. Then his horse was killed and he ended up pinned beneath it, his leg broken. And most historians do believe Arnold helped win the battle.

So Benedict Arnold was for sure a hero at the Battles of Saratoga. But he put officials who would later be in charge of the historic site in a tough spot. Should they honor a guy who was heroic but then became a traitor? The Saratoga National Historical Park decided that Arnold should be honored . . .

sort of. Today at the site, there's a monument to Arnold that doesn't give his name and shows only his wounded leg, with this inscription:

ERECTED 1887 BY JOHN WATTS DE PEYSTER
BREV: MAJ: GEN: S.N.Y. 2ND
V. PRES'T SARATOGA MON'T ASS'T'N:
IN MEMORY OF THE "MOST BRILLIANT SOLDIER"
OF THE CONTINENTAL ARMY, WHO WAS DESPERATELY
WOUNDED ON THIS SPOT, THE SALLY PORT OF
BURGOYNES "GREAT WESTERN REDOUBT"
7TH OCTOBER 1777, WINNING FOR HIS COUNTRYMEN
THE DECISIVE BATTLE OF THE AMERICAN REVOLUTION
AND FOR HIMSELF THE RANK OF MAJOR GENERAL.

The American victory at Saratoga was important for a few reasons. It proved once and for all that American forces could hold their own in a major battle. And more importantly, it convinced the French to join the war. After Saratoga, France recognized America's independence and then declared war on England. The Spanish and Dutch would do the same later on, turning the American Revolution into a world war, with battles fought around the globe.

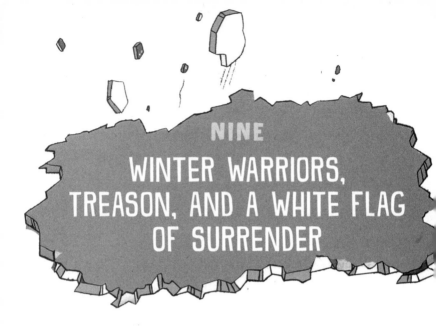

NINE
WINTER WARRIORS, TREASON, AND A WHITE FLAG OF SURRENDER

Saratoga was a major victory for the Continental Army, but the war was far from over. Washington's troops marched to Valley Forge, Pennsylvania, and spent the winter of 1777–1778 camped there. And it wasn't just men holed up at Valley Forge. Along with about twelve thousand soldiers were hundreds of women and children, all crowded into what had become its own city. These families had been traveling with the soldiers, helping out with everything from cooking to sewing to caring for the sick.

Conditions were difficult. There were shortages of food and supplies, and even though smallpox was under control, other diseases like influenza and typhoid raged through the camp. Valley Forge has taken on legendary status in American history. But stories about blustering snowstorms and bitter cold at Valley Forge are more myth than reality. According to primary sources, it didn't snow very often there that winter, and temperatures were often above freezing. It was the following winter, when Washington's army was camped at Morristown, that the temperatures really dropped.

WHAT'S WRONG
WITH THIS PICTURE?

This painting by artist William Trego shows Washington's troops marching to Valley Forge. Trego chose to paint blood in some of the footprints, and that detail is supported by primary sources. In a letter, General William Alexander described the troops as exhausted, saying many were "almost naked, and . . . walking barefooted on the Ice or frozen Ground."

Trego seems to have taken some artistic license with the weather in this scene, though. Emphasizing the harsh conditions, he painted snow falling from the sky and on the ground. But those details made December 19, 1777, look more wintry than it really was. Primary sources described the day as cloudy and rainy rather than snowy.

The fighting heated up again in spring, after Washington learned that the French had arrived to help out. In May 1778, Marquis de Lafayette, who'd come to America from France the year before to join the fight, led a group of men from the Oneida Nation to Philadelphia to find out what the British were planning to do next.

Lafayette's troops met up with the British outside the city at the Battle at Barren Hill. The fighting was short but brutal. It's looked at as a minor battle in the war, but historians give those Oneida soldiers credit for buying time that prevented greater losses to Washington's army.

NATIVE SOLDIERS, TAKING SIDES

Many Native people tried to stay out of the conflict during the American Revolution, but some nations sided with the colonists. They'd fought against the English in the French and Indian War, and relations remained bad. Many hoped things might improve if the colonists won their freedom. In New England, some Native men signed up to be minutemen even before the fighting began. The Marblehead Mariners, that unit of sailors that kept bailing Washington out of tough situations, included Native soldiers as well as African Americans.

Other Native people sided with England, not because of any loyalty to the king but because they thought that offered them the best chance of not losing even more land to colonization. England's Royal Proclamation of 1763 had put some limits on where the colonists could expand their settlements.

Cherokee warriors, who'd already lost a great deal of land to the colonists, attacked frontier settlements early in the war but were defeated by troops from Virginia, Georgia, and the Carolinas.

The Revolution split the six nations of the Haudenosaunee, or Iroquois, Confederacy. The Mohawk people sided with the British, and most Cayuga, Onondaga, and Seneca people eventually joined them. But Oneida and Tuscarora people fought with the Patriots.

In the end, it turned out that Native people couldn't really trust either side. When the British lost the war, they signed a treaty that gave the colonies permission to take even more Native land, and settlers didn't waste any time before they did just that.

In June 1778, British troops abandoned Philadelphia and headed back to try to hold down New York City. On the way, they stopped for a couple of days at Monmouth Courthouse, in New Jersey. When they started out again, leaving behind a small force at the courthouse, Washington ordered General Charles Lee to attack. Lee tried to surround those troops at the courthouse, but more British soldiers arrived, so he retreated instead.

When Washington showed up to help with the battle, he found his men running away. Furious that nobody had told him about the retreat, he rallied his men, got them back in line, and ordered them to fight. The Battle of Monmouth raged on all afternoon, and at the end of the day, it was pretty much a tie. The British took off for New York, and Washington didn't follow them.

WOMEN AT WAR

One of the most famous stories to come out of the Battle of Monmouth was the heroic tale of a woman who held her own on the battlefield after her husband was hurt.

Maybe you've heard the story of brave Molly Pitcher, who stepped up to fire her husband's cannon after he was wounded. She was an inspiration—a great example of courage in the face of danger—and was even honored with her name on a postage stamp in 1928.

But Molly Pitcher wasn't a real person, at least not according to historical documents. Historians believe those "Molly Pitcher" stories were likely about a couple of other real women, named Mary Ludwig Hays and Margaret Corbin. Both took their husbands' places at the cannon after the men were injured in different battles. Molly Pitcher became a symbol of all the women who assisted the Continental Army. Many carried water to the troops (that's where the name Pitcher comes from) and did other jobs to help out, both on the battlefield and off.

Most supported the cause by being camp

followers who trekked around with the army to cook food and do laundry. Others served as spies. But a woman named Deborah Sampson wanted a different role, so she disguised herself as a man and joined the Fourth Massachusetts Regiment, using the fake name Robert Shurtleff. Just where Sampson fought remains a bit of a mystery. When she gave talks about her service after the war, she told action-packed stories about fighting in the Battle of Yorktown, but a recently discovered diary from a man who lived in her town said she enlisted well after that combat took place.

Sampson is believed to have fought in multiple skirmishes, though, one of which ended with a musket ball in her leg. She reportedly refused treatment and dug it out herself so no one would find out who she really was. But in 1783, Sampson got sick with a fever, and a Philadelphia doctor discovered that "Robert Shurtleff" wasn't a man after all. She was given an honorable discharge and eventually fought successfully to get her pension, a payment from the government, as a wounded veteran.

With Boston and Philadelphia lost, the British worked hard on holding ground in the South. Redcoat troops occupied Savannah, Georgia, in December 1778.

Fighting also broke out on the frontier, the area to the west of the colonies. From May to December,

George Rogers Clark commanded a force of frontiersmen to capture several British posts in the Ohio Territory (present-day Illinois and Indiana).

In 1779, more battles were fought in the South, in Georgia and the Carolinas. And in the North, British troops burned Fairfield and Norwalk, Connecticut.

Washington's troops spent the next winter back in Morristown, New Jersey, and conditions there were even more brutal than they'd been at Valley Forge. The winter of 1779–1780 was one of the coldest of the entire eighteenth century. But fewer men died at Morristown than at Valley Forge, perhaps because they were more used to the harsh conditions by then and better at setting up a winter camp.

When spring arrived, the Redcoats set their sights on taking Charleston, South Carolina. By May, British troops were occupying the city. Through the rest of that year, Continental troops suffered numerous defeats in the South, but little by little, they were also chipping away at the British army.

AS THE WAR DRAGGED ON, INFORMATION BECAME EVEN MORE CRUCIAL. BOTH SIDES RELIED ON SPIES TO GATHER SECRETS.

A BRITISH SPY NAMED JOHN ANDRÉ WAS AT THE HEART OF A PLAN TO CAPTURE THE AMERICAN FORT AT WEST POINT, NEW YORK.

ANDRÉ HAD BEEN SECRETLY CORRESPONDING WITH AN AMERICAN OFFICER, WHO'D PROMISED TO HAND OVER THE FORT FOR £20,000.

THAT AMERICAN OFFICER WAS NONE OTHER THAN BENEDICT ARNOLD, WHO'D FOUGHT AS A HERO IN ALL THOSE BATTLES EARLIER IN THE WAR. SO WHAT HAPPENED?

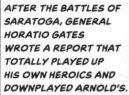

AFTER THE BATTLES OF SARATOGA, GENERAL HORATIO GATES WROTE A REPORT THAT TOTALLY PLAYED UP HIS OWN HEROICS AND DOWNPLAYED ARNOLD'S.

ARNOLD DID EVENTUALLY GET A PROMOTION, BUT HE NEVER GOT OVER BEING ANGRY. SIDELINED BY THE WOUND HE GOT AT SARATOGA, ARNOLD WAS PUT IN COMMAND OF PHILADELPHIA, WHERE HE FELL IN LOVE WITH A LOYALIST NAMED PEGGY SHIPPEN.

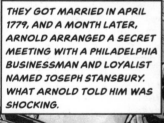

THEY GOT MARRIED IN APRIL 1779, AND A MONTH LATER, ARNOLD ARRANGED A SECRET MEETING WITH A PHILADELPHIA BUSINESSMAN AND LOYALIST NAMED JOSEPH STANSBURY. WHAT ARNOLD TOLD HIM WAS SHOCKING.

HE WANTED TO SPY FOR THE BRITISH.

SOON ARNOLD WAS EXCHANGING LETTERS WITH JOHN ANDRÉ.

HIS PLAN TO BETRAY THE CONTINENTAL ARMY WAS UNDERWAY.

IN AUGUST 1780, ARNOLD TOOK COMMAND OF THE AMERICAN FORT AT WEST POINT. A MONTH LATER, HE MADE A SECRET DEAL WITH ANDRÉ TO HAND IT OVER TO THE BRITISH.

ANDRÉ MET WITH ARNOLD TO FINALIZE THE PLAN AND WAS ON HIS WAY BACK TO NEW YORK CITY WHEN HE WAS CAPTURED BY THREE MILITIAMEN.

WHEN ARNOLD FOUND OUT THAT ANDRÉ HAD BEEN CAPTURED, HE ESCAPED ON A BRITISH SHIP.

THEY FOUND THE PLANS TO WEST POINT HIDDEN IN ANDRÉ'S BOOT.

ANDRÉ WAS HANGED AS A SPY.

Historians believe Benedict Arnold switched sides for a few different reasons: His Loyalist wife introduced him to others who shared her views. Arnold was still bitter about how he'd been treated by the Patriots. He also needed money. And at that time, it looked to Arnold like America might never win independence.

But it turns out, the war was coming to an end. From May to June of 1781, Patriots launched what's now known as the Siege of Ninety Six, an attack on a British garrison in South Carolina that was among the longest sieges of the war. Even though the Patriots weren't successful, it was starting to become clear that the British didn't have enough troops to hold on to all their territory in the South.

In July 1781, General Henry Clinton was commanding British troops in New York City, while in the South, another British general, Lord Cornwallis, was dug in with his men in Yorktown, Virginia. He didn't have a huge army, but he was expecting backup troops from New York soon.

As for the Americans, Washington's troops were camped outside New York City, along with French officer Comte de Rochambeau and his men, hoping for an opportunity to take the city back from the British. They were waiting for help, too—the French fleet that was coming north from the West Indies.

The problem was, Washington and Rochambeau weren't quite sure *where* the French fleet was going to end up. Remember, there were no cell phones back then, so it was a lot harder to keep track of where everybody was and where they were going. Letters had to be carried by messengers, who could be delayed for all kinds of reasons. So it took a while for Washington to figure out that the French fleet wasn't coming to New York after all; it was headed for Chesapeake Bay.

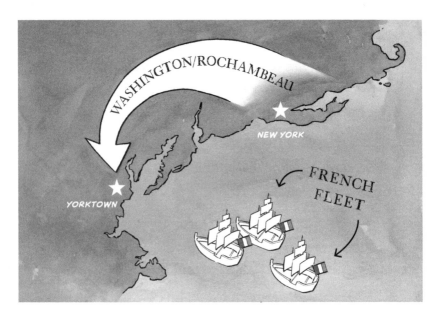

Rochambeau convinced Washington to give up on New York for the time being and head to Virginia instead. But it had to be a secret! So Washington wrote up phony plans for an attack on New York and arranged for them to be leaked to the British.

He even put some of his men to work building an army camp, to give the impression they were getting ready to settle in for the long haul. They built big brick ovens to make it look as if they'd be hanging out for months, baking bread and waiting to attack New York. But really, Washington took most of his troops and his French allies and hightailed it toward Virginia.

In late August, the French fleet arrived in the Chesapeake Bay with twenty-four ships and waited for Washington and Rochambeau to arrive. Washington had already ordered Lafayette to block the British escape from the peninsula by land.

On September 5, the French fleet engaged British ships in the Chesapeake in what's now called the Battle of the Capes. British ships were damaged and sent back to New York for repairs. The French fleet set up a blockade so Cornwallis couldn't get supplies or reinforcements by sea.

Once the American and French troops arrived in late September, Cornwallis was pretty much trapped. More than seventeen thousand American and French troops had arrived in nearby Williamsburg, ready to attack the eighty-three hundred British soldiers at Yorktown.

Cornwallis got word that more troops would arrive October 5. So he ordered his men to dig trenches and build redoubts around Yorktown.

American and French soldiers dug their own trench. They finished on October 9 and started pounding Cornwallis's troops with cannon fire.

In two days, the British guns were knocked out. American and French soldiers had seized two of the British redoubts. Cornwallis was in trouble, and those backup troops from New York were still nowhere to be found.

On October 11, Washington's men advanced. They built another trench, and on the night of October 14, they attacked two more important British redoubts.

Alexander Hamilton, who was commanding one of Washington's battalions, led an advance on one of the British redoubts. And when Cornwallis's soldiers opened fire, Hamilton's men charged in for up-close combat. It was a brutal fight, with bayonets, swords, and hand-to-hand combat.

When it was over, Hamilton had lost 10 percent of his men, the British had lost three quarters of theirs, and the Americans had control of the redoubt. French soldiers had seized the other one, and that was the beginning of the end for Cornwallis. On October 17, he sent out an officer with a white flag, and officers started working out the terms of surrender, which happened two days later.

Normally, that would have been a formal ceremony between commanding officers, with Cornwallis handing over his sword to Washington. But Cornwallis refused to show up. He said he was sick (nobody really believed him; most thought he was being a sore loser) and sent General Charles O'Hara to the surrender ceremony instead.

Washington, who was supposed to accept Cornwallis's sword, decided he wasn't going to accept a sword from someone with a lower rank, so he refused to participate in the ceremony, too, and had his second-in-command, Benjamin Lincoln, accept O'Hara's sword. It was kind of a disappointing surrender after such a long war.

As thousands of British soldiers marched out of Yorktown to lay down their weapons for the surrender, they were flanked by American and French troops. The procession went on for a mile. A British army band played as they marched, and legend says the tune was "The World Turned Upside Down." That would have been appropriate for the moment a bunch of rebel colonists defeated the great British Empire . . . if it were true.

There's no evidence to support that story, though (even though it makes for a really great scene in Lin-Manuel Miranda's Broadway musical *Hamilton*). In reality, no primary sources mention that song.

Nobody even suggested it had been played at the surrender until 1828, so historians think that's probably one of those myths that needs a little smashing.

"THE WORLD TURNED UPSIDE DOWN"

So what about those troops Clinton had promised to send from New York to help Cornwallis? They did eventually arrive, after the British had already surrendered.

TEN
NOW WHAT?

After the surrender at Yorktown, thousands of British troops were taken prisoner. Washington marched his army back to New York for the winter, while the French troops camped out in Virginia. British generals Clinton and Cornwallis sailed back to England and spent years blaming each other for everything that had gone wrong.

SPY ALERT!

JAMES ARMISTEAD

How did the Continental Army manage to overpower the British at Yorktown? Spies had a lot to do with it. One of them was James Armistead, an enslaved man who had enlisted under General Lafayette to help the Continental Army in 1781. Armistead pretended to be a runaway slave, spying on the Americans for the British. And he was apparently a pretty great actor, because General Cornwallis welcomed him into the British camp at Yorktown.

From there, Armistead went back and forth, sharing information with Washington's army. Historians believe his intel helped the Continental Army win the battle—and the war.

The Battle of Yorktown is often talked about as the end of the Revolutionary War, but it really wasn't. There were more skirmishes, and the British continued to occupy New York City and Charleston until the official peace treaty was signed in 1783.

But Yorktown *was* the battle that convinced the British it just wasn't worth it to keep fighting for control of the American colonies. The war had turned out to be so much longer and more expensive than they'd expected. And at the time, the British Empire was busy fighting in other places, too—India, Gibraltar, the West Indies, and Ireland.

So in March 1782, the British Parliament officially voted to give up the fight. Later that year, officials signed a preliminary peace agreement, which led to the signing of the Treaty of Paris, the final agreement to end the war, in September 1783.

American artist Benjamin West created a painting that shows those historic negotiations. Or at least, he tried to. The painting didn't exactly work out because the British commissioners refused to pose for it. So West ended up with half a painting instead.

With the Treaty of Paris, Britain officially recognized America's independence and set boundaries for the new nation.

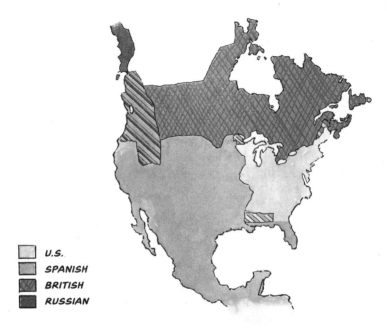

U.S.
SPANISH
BRITISH
RUSSIAN

Don't forget that all of this land being claimed is the traditional homeland of Native people who'd lived on the continent for thousands of years. So why weren't their tribal nations shown on the map? How come it laid out the territorial claims of the United States, Britain, and Spain but never mentioned the Wampanoag, Haudenosaunee, or Cherokee people? And what happened to all those promises the British had made about limiting settlers to protect Native homelands?

If you've learned much at all about how white settlers treated Native people, it probably won't surprise you to know that those promises were broken. Tribes that had fought with the British and those that supported the colonists all found themselves betrayed once again as their traditional homelands were divvied up after the war. The Treaty of Paris made no mention at all of the rights of Native people. Officials of the new United States government didn't honor the treaties the British had made (and they broke a bunch they'd made themselves, too). Even though so many Native people had served with the Continental Army during the war, they were pretty much forgotten as soon as it ended.

African American soldiers who fought in the American Revolution were also betrayed. Remember how the British had promised freedom to enslaved people who escaped from Patriots and joined their cause? That promise fell apart at Yorktown. When Cornwallis found his army trapped and running low on food and supplies, he tossed thousands of Black people who'd been following and supporting his army out of his camp to fend for themselves. Many died of smallpox. Others were captured and enslaved again.

After the battle ended, plantation owners paid soldiers to search the woods for those men who'd been serving with the British. Some officers in the Continental Army even went out themselves, hoping to re-enslave the people who had escaped from them. George Washington found at least two of the African American people who had escaped from him and sent them back to Mount Vernon, where they'd be enslaved for the rest of their lives.

And what about the people who'd been enslaved by Thomas Jefferson, who wrote all those words about the right to life, liberty, and the pursuit of happiness? Thirty enslaved people had escaped Jefferson's plantation to fight with the British. Half of

them died from diseases. After Yorktown, Jefferson recovered about half a dozen of the people he'd enslaved and either sold them or gave them away. He didn't free any of them. No one is sure what happened to the others.

When the United States and Britain were negotiating to officially end the war, Americans demanded that all those enslaved people who'd fought with the British be returned so they could be enslaved again. The British refused, but many of those people ended up enslaved anyway. British Loyalists in the South enslaved thousands. Others were sent to the North, where they struggled to make lives for themselves. But thousands more were sent on ships to the West Indies, where they lived the rest of their lives in slavery.

It was clear by then that America's Black soldiers had been among the very best in the Continental Army. According to the diary of the French baron Ludwig von Closen, about a quarter of the American troops at Yorktown were Black men. He made it a point to praise the First Rhode Island Regiment, which was made up mostly of African Americans.

That regiment is the most neatly dressed, the best under arms, and the most precise in its maneuvers.

You might think this made the Patriots rethink their stance on slavery. But it didn't. Just as African American soldiers who'd fought for the British were often sent right back into slavery, many of those who'd been promised freedom if they fought for the Continental Army ended up enslaved again, too.

Even James Armistead, the spy who helped win the Battle of Yorktown, was re-enslaved after the war. He remained enslaved until 1787, when his former commander, Lafayette, helped petition for his freedom. But still, there was absolutely no protection for African Americans written into America's new government.

That new government had been in the works long before Yorktown. In November 1777, the Continental Congress had approved a document called the Articles of Confederation, a temporary plan for governing the new nation until something more permanent was established. The Articles of Confederation were ratified, or approved, by all thirteen states in March 1781 and remained in effect until America's Constitution went into effect in 1789.

WHAT'S THE REAL DEAL WITH GEORGE WASHINGTON?

As the man who commanded the Continental Army and then served as the new nation's first president, George Washington is probably the most famous American of all time. There are also a lot of legends surrounding him. But just how great a leader was he? It depends who you ask.

Some historians believe Washington didn't act quickly enough when Britain was taking the South, and that led to the loss of Charleston in 1780. Even at the time, Comte de Rochambeau, who commanded the French army in America, seemed to notice this.

Washington ... did not conceive the affairs of the south to be {of} such urgency.

And Thomas Paine (remember, he's the guy who wrote *Common Sense*) claimed that Washington got way more credit for America's victory than he deserved. Paine, who had moved to France after the war, had a whole pile of complaints about Washington by then. So he wrote another pamphlet, called *Letter to George Washington.*

You slept away your time in the field till the finances of the country were completely exhausted, and you have but little share in the glory of the final event.

Many historians believe Washington was a good leader in some ways. He was good at talking to people and convincing men to follow him, which is important if you're battling a huge army. But at the same time Washington was leading that fight for freedom, he was keeping more than a hundred people enslaved on his plantation back home in Virginia. And those people most certainly would have had a different opinion about their enslaver.

Even after Washington was president and northern states were beginning to get rid of slavery, he worked hard to keep people enslaved. Before the United States capital was moved to Washington, DC, George Washington lived and worked in Philadelphia. He brought some of the people he enslaved there as servants. But in 1780, Pennsylvania had passed a law called the Gradual Abolition Act, which said that any enslaved person who entered the state and stayed longer than six months would be freed. Instead of going along with that law, Washington found a sneaky way around it. Every six months, he'd haul the people he enslaved back to his plantation in Virginia or take them on another trip out of the state in order to reset the clock on their freedom. Over and over and over again. Even at the time, Washington seemed to know that was wrong, or at least that people would judge him harshly for it, because he told his personal secretary to keep it a secret.

> I request that these Sentiments and this advise may be known to none but yourself & Mrs. Washington.

Washington's personal character also comes into question with the story of his false teeth. Legend says the first president had wooden teeth, but that's not true. We know now, from scientific analysis, that Washington's false teeth were actually made of ivory (from elephants and/or hippopotamuses), metal alloys, and other people's teeth. There is also evidence to suggest that some of Washington's teeth were yanked out of the mouths of people he enslaved.

This page from Washington's ledger, his list of expenses from May 1784, shows that he paid six pounds and two shillings to "Negroes for 9 Teeth on Acct. of Dr Lemoin."

Those "Negroes" were what Washington called the people he enslaved. It is true that in those days, it wasn't uncommon for desperately poor or enslaved people to sell their teeth to a dentist, to be used in false teeth for wealthier people. But it's also true that if you were enslaved by the president of the United States, you probably wouldn't have had any choice about whether to have your teeth pulled.

That story about Washington doesn't show up in many history books for kids, probably because it's so horrifying to think about. Especially since George Washington has been lifted up as an American hero. Towns, parks, streets, and schools are named after him. The country gave him a national holiday and put his face on the dollar bill. Many white people really don't like to talk about how Washington treated the people he enslaved.

The problem with that is that it erases part of America's history.

More than one thing can be true. It's true that

George Washington led the Continental Army to victory, resulting in American independence. It is also true that he enslaved people, treated them cruelly, and continued to support laws that kept slavery alive after he was president. Because of that, slavery and inequality would become as much a part of America's legacy as the Revolution itself.

Most of America's early presidents enslaved people. So it's fair to say that their ideas about liberty were pretty messed up. The truth is, the men who launched the American Revolution didn't really know what they were getting into. They were imperfect men who had some really imperfect ideas about freedom. And they had doubts themselves. Would this whole independence thing work out? They weren't sure, even after the Revolution was won. Would American people be too greedy and worried about their own interests to work together for the good of the country? It's a question many would say remains unanswered.

But maybe what's most interesting about the Declaration of Independence is how it went on to inspire movements that the Founders couldn't have imagined. Those words—that promise about life, liberty, and the pursuit of happiness—would be used later on to successfully fight for freedom for African Americans, and for voting rights for women, Native people, and people of color. The Declaration of Independence continues to spark fights for change in America even today, as citizens work together to make that new nation born out of the American Revolution stronger and fairer for everyone.

A TIMELINE OF THE AMERICAN REVOLUTION

1733—England passes the Molasses Act, taxing molasses, sugar, and rum from non-British colonies.

1754–63—The French and Indian War results in a victory for England but also a lot of debt.

1764—England passes the Sugar Act and the Currency Act.

1765—England passes the Stamp Act and the Quartering Act.

The Sons of Liberty organize for secret meetings to fight the Stamp Act.

Patriot Stephen Hopkins writes a pamphlet called *The Grievances of the American Colonies, Candidly Examined.*

1766—England passes the Declaratory Act.

1767—England passes the Townshend Acts.

1770—British troops clash with colonists in Boston, and shots are fired, killing three colonists and wounding eight more (two of whom would later die), in what would come to be known as the Boston Massacre.

1772

June—Patriots loot and burn a British ship off Rhode Island, in what's come to be known as the Gaspee Affair.

1773

June—England passes the Tea Act.

December—The Sons of Liberty and other Patriots board British ships in Boston Harbor and dump hundreds of cartons of tea overboard in what's now called the Boston Tea Party.

1774—England passes the Coercive Acts, also known as the Intolerable Acts. In response, the colonies come together for the First Continental Congress, and the colonies start to prepare for a possible war.

1775

April—British general Thomas Gage is ordered to take steps to crush the rebellion in the colonies. British troops are told to capture rebel leaders in Lexington and destroy colonial supplies in Concord. Colonists fight Redcoat soldiers in the battles at Lexington and Concord.

May—Ethan Allen and Benedict Arnold lead militias to capture Fort Ticonderoga from the British.

The Second Continental Congress talks about the possibility of declaring independence from Great Britain, but most members are still in favor of trying to work things out.

June—The Battle of Bunker Hill breaks out in Charlestown. Redcoat soldiers eventually win, but they suffer heavy losses.

July—George Washington takes command of the Continental Army.

November—Continental Army troops occupy Montreal.

The Continental Congress bans African American men from serving in the Continental Army.

England offers freedom to enslaved men who escape from Patriot masters to fight with the British.

December—General Richard Montgomery and Benedict Arnold are defeated by British forces while trying to take Quebec.

Patriot forces attack Loyalists in the Carolinas and Virginia.

Washington announces a change to Continental Army policy; African American men will be allowed to serve as soldiers.

1776

January—Thomas Paine publishes *Common Sense,* which urges the colonies to seek independence and gains support for the idea.

Henry Knox arrives in Boston with his men and the cannons they dragged through the snow all the way from Fort Ticonderoga.

February—Patriots defeat a group of Loyalists at the Battle of Moore's Creek Bridge in North Carolina.

March—The Continental Army places cannons on a hill overlooking Boston and forces the British to evacuate the city.

May—The Continental Congress passes a resolution urging colonies to set up their own governments.

June—Richard Henry Lee of Virginia proposes to the Continental Congress that the colonies declare themselves to be "free and independent States." The resolution doesn't get approved that day, but the Congress appoints a committee to write a statement about independence in case support for it grows.

Thomas Jefferson collaborates with John Adams and Benjamin Franklin to write a draft of the Declaration of Independence, which is then revised by other members of the Continental Congress.

British forces try to take Charleston, South Carolina, but are defeated by Patriots at Sullivan's Island.

July—English ships arrive in New York Harbor.

The Continental Congress votes to approve Richard Henry Lee's resolution for independence, then approves the final text of the Declaration of Independence and sends it off to be printed.

August—British troops seize Brooklyn, but Washington's army is saved by the Marblehead Mariners, who ferry soldiers across the East River to escape.

September—American spy Nathan Hale is captured and executed by the British.

October—Benedict Arnold's fleet fights the British on Lake Champlain in the Battle of Valcour Island.

November—After the British take western Long Island, Manhattan, Staten Island, and more of the Hudson Valley, Washington's troops retreat to Pennsylvania.

December—On Christmas night, Washington's army crosses the Delaware River to launch a surprise attack on Trenton, which is occupied by Hessian soldiers. The Continental Army wins a much-needed victory.

1777

January—Continental troops defeat British soldiers in the Battle of Princeton before setting up camp in Morristown, New Jersey, for the winter.

April—Benedict Arnold leads troops to push back the British in Ridgefield, Connecticut.

July—British troops take back Fort Ticonderoga.

August—The British abandon Fort Stanwix in New York.

Continental troops defeat the British at the Battle of Bennington.

British troops defeat Continental soldiers at the Battle of Oriskany.

September—The Battle of Brandywine, one of the bloodiest clashes of the war, ends with a British victory and heavy casualties on both sides.

Washington retreats after a conflict in the rain in the Battle of the Clouds.

British troops occupy Philadelphia.

September–October—The Continental Army defeats British troops in the Battles of Saratoga.

November—The Continental Congress approves the Articles of Confederation, a temporary plan for American self-government.

December—Washington's troops march to Valley Forge and set up winter camp.

1778

February—France joins the war on the side of the Patriots.

May—Marquis de Lafayette leads Oneida soldiers to Philadelphia, and they fight the British in the Battle of Barren Hill.

From May to December, George Rogers Clark leads a campaign to capture British posts in the Ohio Territory (now Illinois and Indiana).

June—British troops abandon Philadelphia and head for New York City. On the way, Continental troops attack them, leading to the Battle of Monmouth, which ends with the British retreating to New York and Washington's army staying behind.

December—British troops occupy Savannah.

1779

December—Washington's troops set up camp in Morristown, New Jersey, and endure a winter even colder and snowier than Valley Forge.

1780

May—British troops take Charleston.

September—Benedict Arnold makes a secret deal to turn West Point over to the British. He's discovered when a British spy named John André is captured with the plans hidden in his boot. Arnold flees to a British ship, and André is executed as a spy.

October—Patriot militias defeat Loyalists at Kings Mountain, South Carolina.

1781

January—The Continental Army defeats the British at the Battle of Cowpens in South Carolina.

March—British forces defeat Continental soldiers—but also lose a lot of men—at the Battle of Guilford Courthouse in North Carolina.

All thirteen states ratify the Articles of Confederation.

May–June—Patriot forces attack British troops in the Siege of Ninety Six in South Carolina.

September–October—With the help of the French, the Continental Army surrounds the British and defeats them at the Battle of Yorktown.

1783

September—The Treaty of Paris is signed, officially ending the Revolutionary War.

AUTHOR'S NOTE

When I was growing up in Western New York, the stories I learned about the American Revolution were all pretty similar—about how the brave colonists rallied to beat the British army so America could be a new nation. Our textbooks showed paintings of Continental Army generals in sparkling uniforms, claiming victory on the battlefield. They were the heroes of history; bossy old King George and his nasty Redcoat soldiers were the villains. Native people and African Americans who fought on both sides were most often left out of the story entirely.

But as I grew older and read more about history, I came to understand that people from the past are almost never as simple and clear-cut as legends make them out to be. That includes men like George Washington and Thomas Jefferson, who spoke so eloquently about freedom but also enslaved people and continued to do so as long as they were alive. And it includes the so-called villains of history, too, like the Hessian soldiers, who were painted as heartless brutes, when really they were mostly poor young men who thought America seemed like a promising place for a future. It also includes the Revolution's most notorious traitor, Benedict Arnold.

It was only years later, after I moved to Northern New York, that I learned the rest of Arnold's story. I live just a few miles from the site of the Battle of Valcour Island, on a lake where Revolutionary War cannonballs still rest deep in the mud beneath the surface. From my kitchen window, I can see the bay where Arnold anchored the Continental fleet, waiting to engage British ships. I was amazed when I first heard the story of that battle and how Arnold led the fleet to escape in the dark. How had I never known about this, or about Arnold's heroics during the Battles of Saratoga?

The truth is, stories that don't fit the patriotic

myth of how America came to be have often been ignored or set to the side, even when the historical documents that support them are clear. The story of the American Revolution is the founding story of the entire nation, and sometimes people opt for patriotism instead of facts when they're telling that story. They'd rather talk about legendary good guys and bad guys than imperfect heroes and villains who were heroic before they became infamous traitors.

But the problem with retelling those myths is that it doesn't allow us to learn from what actually happened. That's why I'm most grateful to the team at Random House and everyone who helped make this series of books a reality. For this installment, I'm especially grateful to the staff of the Museum of the American Revolution in Philadelphia, the Smithsonian Museum of American History and Museum of African American History and Culture, and Washington Crossing Historic Park for research help, and to all of my early readers.

Here are some resources to explore if you'd like to learn more about the real stories of the American Revolution.

BOOKS

American Revolution (DK Eyewitness Books) by Stuart Murray
(DK Children, 2015)

Answering the Cry for Freedom: Stories of African Americans and the American Revolution by Gretchen Woelfle; illustrated by R. Gregory Christie (Calkins Creek, 2016)

George Washington, Spymaster: How the Americans Outspied the British and Won the Revolutionary War by Thomas B. Allen (National Geographic, 2007)

Ona Judge Outwits the Washingtons: An Enslaved Woman Fights for Freedom by Gwendolyn Hooks; illustrated by Simone Agoussoye (Capstone, 2019)

The Real Benedict Arnold by Jim Murphy (Clarion Books, 2007)

A Spy Called James: The True Story of James Lafayette, Revolutionary War Double Agent by Anne Rockwell; illustrated by Floyd Cooper (Carolrhoda Books, 2016)

HISTORICAL SITES AND MUSEUMS

Many of the battle sites and other locations in this book are now historical sites with visitor centers and museums that you can visit with your family. Their websites also include excellent resources for learning more about the American Revolution.

Boston's Freedom Trail includes the Paul Revere House, the Old North Church, the Bunker Hill Monument, and other sites related to the American Revolution.

thefreedomtrail.org

Minute Man National Historical Park, in Massachusetts, lets visitors explore the people and places involved in the battles at Lexington and Concord.

nps.gov/mima

Fort Ticonderoga, still standing in Northern New York, is now a historical site and museum.

fortticonderoga.org

Saratoga National Historical Park, in upstate New York, includes a visitor center, monuments, and trails that let visitors explore the battle sites.

nps.gov/sara

Independence National Historical Park, in Philadelphia, includes several museums as well as Independence Hall, where the Declaration of Independence was signed, and the Liberty Bell.

nps.gov/inde

Philadelphia's Museum of the American Revolution has many exhibits that tell the story of the war and the people who fought it.

amrevmuseum.org

Washington Crossing Historic Park is in Pennsylvania, on the Delaware River, where George Washington and his troops crossed to attack Trenton.

washingtoncrossingpark.org

Valley Forge National Historical Park, in Pennsylvania, commemorates the Continental Army's winter encampment of 1777–1778.

nps.gov/vafo

Guilford Courthouse National Military Park, in North Carolina, has a visitor center, trails, and a tour road, where guests can learn more about the battle that took place there.

nps.gov/guco

Cowpens National Battlefield, in South Carolina, has a visitor center and trails that allow guests to explore the site of the battle.

nps.gov/cowp

Colonial National Historical Park, in Virginia, includes visitor centers at the Yorktown Battlefield and Jamestowne Island, one of the first colonial settlements.

nps.gov/colo

This interactive website from the National Park Service has a collection of other Revolutionary War historical sites.

nps.gov/subjects/americanrevolution/visit.htm

SELECTED BIBLIOGRAPHY

Aron, Paul. *We Hold These Truths . . . and Other Words That Made America.* Lanham, MD: Rowman & Littlefield, 2008.

Balderston, Marion, and David Syrett, eds. *The Lost War: Letters from British Officers During the American Revolution.* New York: Horizon Press, 1975.

Bellico, Russell P. *Sails and Steam in the Mountains: A Maritime and Military History of Lake George and Lake Champlain.* Fleischmanns, NY: Purple Mountain Press, 1992.

Blakemore, Erin. "George Washington Used Legal Loopholes to Avoid Freeing His Slaves." *Smithsonian Magazine.* February 16, 2015. smithsonianmag.com/smart-news/george-washington-used -legal-loopholes-avoid-freeing-his-slaves-180954283.

Brown, Peter. "June 25, 1775 Letter from Peter Brown to His Mother," Massachusetts Historical Society, masshist.org/bh/brownp3text .html.

Chernow, Ron. *Washington: A Life.* New York: Penguin Press, 2010.

Crews, Ed. "The Truth about Betsy Ross: Popular Lore Says She Made First Flag, but Evidence for the Tale Is Scarce." *Colonial Williamsburg Journal,* Summer 2008. research.colonialwilliamsburg.org/ Foundation/journal/Summer08/betsy.cfm.

Daigler, Kenneth A. *Spies, Patriots, and Traitors: American Intelligence in the Revolutionary War.* Washington, DC: Georgetown University Press, 2014.

Duffy, John J., and H. Nicholas Muller III. *Inventing Ethan Allen.* Lebanon, NH: University Press of New England, 2014.

Egerton, Douglas R. *Death or Liberty: African Americans and Revolutionary America.* New York: Oxford University Press, 2009.

Ellis, Joseph J. *Revolutionary Summer: The Birth of American Independence.* New York: Vintage Books, 2013.

Fenn, Elizabeth A. *Pox Americana: The Great Smallpox Epidemic of 1775–82.* New York: Hill and Wang, 2001.

Ferling, John. "Myths of the American Revolution: A Noted Historian Debunks the Conventional Wisdom about America's War of Independence." *Smithsonian Magazine,* January 2010. smithsonianmag.com/history/myths-of-the-american -revolution-10941835.

Ferling, John. *Whirlwind: The American Revolution and the War that Won It.* New York: Bloomsbury, 2015.

Gilbert, Alan. *Black Patriots and Loyalists: Fighting for Emancipation in the War for Independence.* Chicago: University of Chicago Press, 2012.

Greenberg, David. "The Nation; Debunking America's Enduring Myths." *New York Times*, June 29, 2003. nytimes.com/2003/06 /29/weekinreview/the-nation-debunking-america-s-enduring -myths.html.

Handwerk, Brian. "4th of July: Nine Myths Debunked." *National Geographic News*, July 4, 2012. nationalgeographic.com /news/2012/7/120704-4th-of-july-fourth-myths-google-doodle -nation-independence-day.

Hinderaker, Eric. *Boston's Massacre*. Cambridge, MA: Belknap Press of Harvard University Press, 2017.

Katz, Brigit. "Diary Sheds Light on Deborah Sampson, Who Fought in the Revolutionary War." *Smithsonian Magazine*. July 2, 2019. smithsonianmag.com/smart-news/diary-sheds-light-deborah -sampson-who-fought-revolutionary-war-180972547.

Ketchum, Richard M. *The Winter Soldiers*. New York: Doubleday, 1973.

Lengel, Edward G., ed. *This Glorious Struggle: George Washington's Revolutionary War Letters*. New York: HarperCollins, 2007.

Maier, Pauline. *American Scripture: Making the Declaration of Independence*. New York: Alfred A. Knopf, 1997.

Maier, Pauline. *From Resistance to Revolution: Colonial Radicals and the Development of American Opposition to Britain, 1765–1776*. New York: W. W. Norton, 1991.

McCullough, David. *1776*. New York: Simon & Schuster, 2005.

Misencik, Paul R. *The Original American Spies: Seven Covert Agents of the Revolutionary War*. Jefferson, NC: McFarland, 2014.

Mount Vernon. "George Washington and Slave Teeth." George Washington's Mount Vernon. mountvernon.org/george -washington/health/washingtons-teeth/george-washington -and-slave-teeth.

Nagy, John A. *George Washington's Secret Spy War: The Making of America's First Spymaster*. New York: St. Martin's Press, 2016.

Nash, Gary B. *The Forgotten Fifth: African Americans in the Age of Revolution*. Cambridge, MA: Harvard University Press, 2006.

Nash, Gary B., and Graham Russell Gao Hodges. *Friends of Liberty: Thomas Jefferson, Tadeusz Kosciuszko, and Agrippa Hull*. New York: Basic Books, 2008.

National Park Service. "Saratoga National Historic Park: History & Culture." nps.gov/sara/learn/historyculture.

Nelson, Craig. *Thomas Paine: Enlightenment, Revolution, and the Birth of Modern Nations*. New York: Penguin Books, 2007.

Newell, Margaret Ellen. *Brethren by Nature: New England Indians, Colonists, and the Origins of American Slavery*. Ithaca, NY: Cornell University Press, 2015.

Northumberland, Hugh Percy, Duke of. *Letters of Hugh, Earl Percy, from Boston and New York, 1774–1776*. Edited by Charles Knowles Bolton. Boston: C. E. Goodspeed, 1902. lccn.loc.gov/02017871.

Oneida Indian Nation. "The Battle at Barren Hill." oneidaindiannation.com/the-battle-at-barren-hill.

Paine, Thomas. "Letter to George Washington." Thomas Paine National Historical Association. thomaspaine.org/major-works /letter-to-george-washington.html.

Parkinson, Robert G. *The Common Cause: Creating Race and Nation in the American Revolution.* Chapel Hill: University of North Carolina Press, 2016.

Perkins, Russell S. "Yorktown Campaign." Mount Vernon. mountvernon.org/library/digitalhistory/digital-encyclopedia /article/yorktown-campaign.

Phillips, Kevin. *1775: A Good Year for Revolution.* New York: Penguin Books, 2012.

Rakove, Jack. *Revolutionaries: A New History of the Invention of America.* Boston: Houghton Mifflin Harcourt, 2010.

Raphael, Ray. *Founding Myths: Stories That Hide Our Patriotic Past.* New York: New Press, 2004.

Schocket, Andrew M. *Fighting over the Founders: How We Remember the American Revolution.* New York: New York University Press, 2015.

Stelle Smith, Samuel. *The Battle of Trenton.* Monmouth Beach, NJ: Philip Freneau Press, 1965.

Thomas Jefferson Foundation. "Monticello: Slavery FAQs—Property." monticello.org/slavery/slavery-faqs/property.

Travers, Len. *Celebrating the Fourth: Independence Day and the Rites of Nationalism in the Early Republic.* Amherst: University of Massachusetts Press, 1997.

Tsesis, Alexander. *For Liberty and Equality: The Life and Times of the Declaration of Independence.* New York: Oxford University Press, 2012.

Washington, George. "From George Washington to Samuel Washington, 18 December 1776." National Archives. founders .archives.gov/documents/Washington/03-07-02-0299.

Wood, Gordon S. *The Radicalism of the American Revolution.* New York: Vintage Books, 1991.

Yorktown Battlefield. "History of the Siege." nps.gov/york/learn /historyculture/history-of-the-siege.htm.

Young, Alfred F. *Liberty Tree: Ordinary People and the American Revolution.* New York: New York University Press, 2006.

IMAGE CREDITS

Americasroof/Wikimedia Commons (p. 146); Digital Maps Collection/Boston Public Library (p. 110); courtesy of the John Carter Brown Library (p. 28); Library of Congress, George Washington Ledger B (p. 187); Library of Congress, LC-DIG-ppmsca-01657 (p. 21); Library of Congress, LC-USZ62-72497 (p. 67); Library of Congress, LC-USZC4-2791 (p. 134); Library of Congress, LC-USZC4-5315 (p. 40); Library of Congress, mtj.mtjbib000262 (p. 87); Lilly Library/Indiana University Bloomington (p. 113); Massachusetts Historical Society, Boston (pp. 23, 24, 96); Metropolitan Museum of Art (p. 123); Dr. Fred Murphy, Sylvia Whitfield/Centers for Disease Control and Prevention (p. 129); Museum of the American Revolution (p. 150); National Archives (111-SC-94758) (p. 63); National Archives (111-SC-96740) (p. 132); National Archives (111-SC-100815) (p. 73); National Archives (148-GW-923) (p. 155); National Portrait Gallery (p. 72); New York Public Library (p. 52); Pennsylvania Academy of the Fine Arts (p. 82); US Capitol (p. 92); US Government/Wikimedia Commons (p. 156); gift of Howland S. Warren/Museum of Fine Arts Boston (p. 66); Winterthur Museum and County Estate (p. 175); Yale University Art Gallery (p. 83).

INDEX

SMASH MORE STORIES!

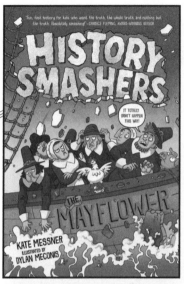

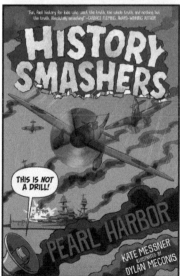

AND COMING SOON!

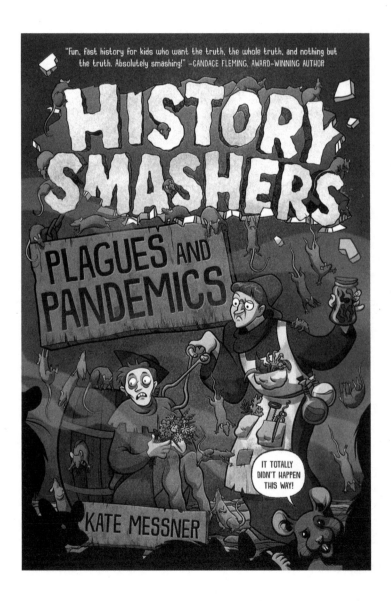